Twin Flames

Love Yourself
And Manifest Ultimate Love

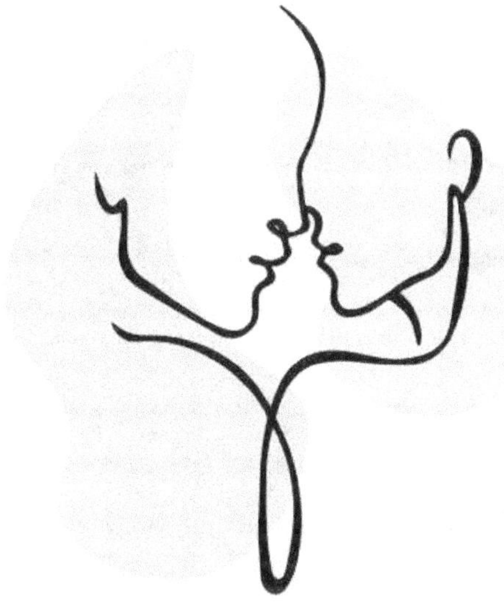

Complete Guide with Exercises,
for Karmic Healing and Law of Attraction

TEMPLUM DİANAE

- MEDİA -

Work edited by: "Templum Dianae Media."
Illustrations and cover art by: "Templum Dianae Media"
Layout and formatting by: "Templum Dianae Media"
Back page and introduction edited by: "Templum Dianae Media"

2024 - All Rights Reserved

---

www.templumdianae.co

İNDEX

Contents

THE JOURNEY OF THE TWIN FLAMES

The journey of the Twin Flames is not like any other. It is not a simple story of love or attraction. It is a deep call, a whisper that passes through you like a warm breeze on a silent night. It surprises you, it shakes you, and before you can understand, you feel a connection that goes beyond what is visible. It is not just a feeling: it is a certainty that lives inside you.

Maybe it has already happened to you. You met someone and the world around you stopped. It wasn't the sound of the words or the look of them, but something deeper. As if, for a moment, time decided not to matter anymore, and all that existed was that moment, that connection. Your heart shuddered, your skin lit up as if run through by a current. You felt a presence, as if that person had always been a part of you, always and forever.

Every day we come across faces, stories, glances. Some slip away like sand between our fingers, others remain, tracing scars or leaving caresses. But then there is that encounter that you do not forget, that marks a "before" and an "after" in your existence. That encounter could be your Twin Flame.

Or maybe not.

Some people say that there is "the one" out there. But what if I told you that it's not just a matter of finding someone who completes you? That the real journey is much deeper than that? Twin Flames is something different, a bond that goes beyond time and space, a karmic dance that intertwines and collides to bring out the true essence of who you are. It is not just love. It is awakening, it is transformation. The road to your Twin Flame is anything but easy. It is not a stroll through a flower garden, but rather a winding path dotted with challenges, pain and, most importantly, growth. Each step you take will lead you to look within, explore your deepest fears, and heal the wounds you have carried with you for lifetimes.

In these pages, you will not find a recipe for perfect love or promises of instant happiness. But you will find a guide, an invisible thread that will lead you through the mystery of your soul. You will feel as if immersed in a new skin, walk between different worlds, cross thresholds you never thought existed.

Feel the energy around you. It is like a gentle pressure on your soul, a call that you cannot ignore. The journey to your Twin Flame will lead you to dissolve the shadows that surround you, burn away old patterns and be reborn. Eventually, you will return to yourself, but you will not be the same. You will be more aware, stronger, and ready to welcome that connection that has been waiting for you forever.

This book is not just to be read: it is to be experienced. Every word, every reflection is an invitation to let go, to lose yourself and find yourself. And when you have passed through the last portal, with a purified heart and an enlightened soul, you will know that it is not fate that decides for you. It is you who creates the path to your spiritual love.

Are you ready to get started?

THE DUALITY OF MAN: BALANCING THE MASCULINE AND FEMININE

Inside each of us lives a deep dualism. It is like a subtle interplay of light and shadow, creating a complex balance between masculine and feminine energy. These two forces, which appear to be opposites, are actually complementary and feed off each other, like day and night, like the sun and the moon. **To find true love and experience deep relationships, you must first harmonize these energies within yourself.**

The Power of Yin and Yang: Understanding Duality

Inside you exist two primordial forces, the Yin and the Yang, constantly dancing in balance, guiding your every choice and feeling. **The Yin is the welcoming energy that retreats into the dark depths of your soul, silent as the night, mysterious as the moon.** It is the part of you that holds the secrets of your innermost emotions, those that resonate with your heartbeats and vibrate beneath the surface.

On the other hand, **Yang is the fire that burns within you**, that drive that makes you act, create, shine like the sun in the clearest sky. It is the force that guides you toward the manifestation of your dreams, the light that brightens your path. As Yin plunges into reflection, Yang bursts into action.

These two principles are never in conflict; rather, they support each other. When **Yin and Yang come together** in balance, you feel an inner peace that allows you to fully embrace who you are and who you are becoming. *Think of the moment when the sun sets and the moon rises-a moment of perfect harmony, where light and shadow meet.*

When Yin calls to you, it invites you to dive within, to look into the shadows and find hidden wisdom, while **Yang urges you to take action, to turn dreams into reality,** bringing with it the clarity and strength to face the world. Duality becomes your power: it completes you, balances you, makes you more aware of the journey you are on toward love, toward your twin flame.

The challenge lies in recognizing when Yin or Yang is out of balance within you. Perhaps you feel overwhelmed by Yang energy, always on the move, without finding a moment of calm. Or perhaps you have allowed yourself to be lulled too much by Yin, losing the courage to act. **The secret is to listen to your heart, to sense when it is time to retreat and when it is time to move forward.**

Yin and Yang are like a breath: the natural rhythm of life, a cycle of expansion and contraction that keeps you in balance. Whenever you let them flow through you, you find the peace and strength you need to grow, love and connect to your soul mate.

The Inner Sun: Exploring the Masculine Principle

Inside you, there is a force that shines like the sun, an energy that drives you to move, to take control, to protect and to build. **This is the masculine principle**, a flame that gives you courage and determination, that drives you to shape the world around you. It is the energy of action, that inner spark that makes you act with clarity and decision.

Feel it growing inside you, like a rising heat, a fire that will not go out. Just as the sun illuminates everything it touches, your soul, when activated by the masculine principle, has the ability to bring light and clarity to every corner of your life. This power is expressed not only in physical strength or determination, but also in the ability to establish boundaries and create structures that protect and support you.

The sun inside you reminds you that no matter how strong your desire to protect and act, there is a need for **balance**. A sun that is too hot burns, while a sun that is too weak does not illuminate enough. **The true power of the masculine principle lies in finding the right balance between strength and gentleness**. It is the courage to act, yes, but also the wisdom to know when to stop, when to leave room for silence and reflection.

Just like the sun rising every day, **your masculine power can be a constant source of energy and stability**, but only if you use it with respect toward yourself and others. **Feel like the sun that is not afraid to shine, but knows the value of its light**.

The Inner Moon: Embracing the Feminine Principle

Within you, shines a light that does not blind, but gently illuminates the path.

This is the feminine energy, the side of your soul that welcomes, nurtures and senses deeply. **Like the moon that regulates the tides, the feminine principle connects you to your deepest emotions**, your intuition, and that mystery that lurks in the unseen. It is not a chaotic or weak force, but a silent power that allows you to flow with events, adapt to circumstances, and trust the design of the universe.

Your inner Moon does not follow strict rules, is not limited to the boundaries drawn by logic or rationality.

On the contrary, it dances beyond those barriers, exploring invisible territories made up of emotions and sensations. It is the energy that allows you to listen to that silent voice inside you, the one that knows without explaining, that hears without needing to see. *It is the whisper that guides you when everything seems uncertain.*

Embracing the feminine principle means allowing yourself to be vulnerable, to open up without fear, knowing that in that vulnerability lies immense strength. It is the courage to show yourself as you are, to flow with challenges and to let your intuition guide you.

Just like the cyclically changing moon, **your feminine energy teaches you that it is in the mutability that true wisdom is found.**

The feminine principle invites you to let go of control, to allow the universe to take its course. You don't always have to struggle to be strong; **sometimes your real strength lies in being soft, in gently welcoming your emotions,** just as the moon welcomes each phase of its cycle without resistance.

While the sun of the masculine principle urges you to create, to build, **the moon guides you to explore mystery,** to find beauty in the shadows, to trust what you cannot see but only perceive.

Your inner moon invites you to dance with the invisible, to embrace every part of yourself, unafraid of what you will discover in the depths of your being.

14

THE WOUNDS OF THE SOUL - HEALING THE SCARS OF THE PAST

Every soul carries scars that tell stories of pain, disappointments, and unresolved trauma. These wounds, often hidden in the depths of the heart, manifest themselves in current relationships, creating obstacles that seem insurmountable. **To truly open yourself to the love of your twin flame, it is necessary to confront and heal these wounds**. When you meet your twin flame, there is no hiding anymore: it is as if every wound, every unhealed scar, reveals itself, demanding attention and healing.

Feeling that pain resurfacing can seem frightening. It's like a fire burning inside you, awakening old emotions you thought you had overcome. **But in that burning, there is also the promise of transformation**. Feel it, experience it, and then let it transform into wisdom. It is a process that frees you, makes you stronger, and brings you closer to harmony with yourself and your twin flame.

The masculine principle within you is related to strength, determination and control. However, when this principle is unbalanced, **its shadows manifest in the form of aggression, fear of showing vulnerability and a constant need to control everything**. These shadows are nothing more than unhealed wounds, traces of pains that are still looking for a way out.

When the masculine succeeds in healing, it becomes a powerful but gentle presence, a force that does not crush but protects and supports. **You will feel a sense of inner security**, a balance between action and patience, and understand that true power is not in control, but in the ability to act without fear.

The feminine principle, connected to sensitivity, caring and intuition, can be deeply wounded when it lacks self-confidence. **When imbalanced, the feminine can become manipulative, insecure and dependent on the approval of others**. This creates a vicious cycle in which the fear of not being enough takes control and stifles your true essence.

Healing the feminine means rediscovering the power of your authenticity, learning to nurture yourself without waiting for the love and approval of others. **Only when the feminine principle is at peace can it create a space of unconditional love,** a space where you can be totally yourself without having to try to fit in or please.

The journey to healing your wounds is not just about healing a part of you. **It is about merging these two opposing energies, masculine and feminine, into a sacred harmony**. When the two forces come together, they create a powerful balance within you. This balance prepares you to meet your twin flame, to welcome that pure love that reflects you completely.

Feel the masculine and feminine energy merge within you, creating a harmony that makes you ready for the most intense and sacred love of your life. When you are in balance, reunion with your twin flame will become inevitable, because you will finally be ready for a union that goes beyond the body and mind to touch the soul.

The Shadows of the Masculine: Healing the Wounds of the Masculine Principle

The masculine principle within you can become a place of disharmony when it is ruled by ego or the constant need for control.

Shadows of the masculine manifest when the energy is not balanced, creating a flow of aggression, resistance to vulnerability, and a deep inability to really listen.

These are old wounds, rooted in past experiences, in hurts that have never been resolved.

Imagine the male principle as a tired warrior.

He fought for a long time, protected and built, but on this journey he got lost, forgetting how to be at peace.

This energy, when wounded, clams up, unable to open up to love or allow itself to be vulnerable. The result is a constant need to defend its space, put up walls and keep everything under control.

But these wounds can be healed. When you begin to bring awareness to the shadows of the masculine, when you recognize those parts of you that try to dominate or control for fear of being wounded, then a path to healing opens. The key is to allow the masculine to relax, to accept that not everything needs to be forcefully protected.

When the masculine principle finds peace, it transforms into a force that nurtures and protects without suffocating. It is like a tree with deep roots, providing shade and shelter, never asking for anything in return.

In this state, it becomes a stable and secure presence, able to support your growth without dominating.

The balanced masculine is the backbone of love and protection, not a force that constrains or limits, but one that embraces and encourages.

Feeling this transformation is like sensing the wind changing direction, gentle and powerful at the same time. **Inside you, when the masculine is healed, it becomes a beacon of light**, a force that guides and supports you on your soul's journey.

Shadows of the Feminine: Healing the Wounded Feminine Principle

The feminine principle, when wounded, can become a dark force that holds you back, making you feel small and dependent on others. **The shadows of the feminine manifest themselves in the form of insecurity, constant need for approval, and emotional manipulation**. It is a dangerous dance, in which your inner power is stifled by the desire to be accepted and loved at all costs. This wounding, rooted in past trauma, painful relationships, or lack of self-esteem, can lead you to seek validation from the outside, forgetting that **true strength lies within**.

When the feminine principle is imbalanced, it tends to control situations out of fear of being abandoned or rejected. It clings to the idea that only the love of others can give you value, and so you end up sacrificing your authenticity to be what you think others want. **It is a painful cycle** that pulls you away from your true inner power, making the feminine a shadow of what it could be.

But **healing the wounded feminine** is possible. Healing begins the moment you allow yourself to **love yourself unconditionally**, to embrace every part of yourself, with no more judgment. This unconditional love is not only toward others, but first of all toward you. It means learning to flow with life, without wanting to control or manipulate it, without fear of losing what is meant for you.

Feel the power of this inner love that does not demand confirmation from the outside. When the wounded feminine heals, it becomes a creative force, an inexhaustible source of nourishment, compassion and insight. **In this space of peace,**

you can allow yourself to be vulnerable and strong at the same time, to welcome the world with your sensitivity without fear of being hurt.

When you begin to heal the feminine principle, **you open yourself to the energy of unconditional love**. This is where the true power of the feminine lies: in the ability to welcome every part of you, even those you have tried to hide or forget. Only then, through this deep healing, **can you prepare to welcome your twin flame**, no longer with the fear of being hurt, but with the courage to love authentically.

The harmonious fusion of the masculine and feminine principles is the final step in achieving wholeness. In you, these two forces intertwine, balance and support each other, creating a sacred space in which you can grow and prepare for the most important encounter of your life: union with your twin flame.

WHAT ARE THE TWIN FLAMES?

Have you ever felt that sudden chill, a deep shock that starts in the heart and runs through the soul? The world seems to stop, and in that moment everything seems clearer. His presence awakens something ancient, a bond that transcends time and space. It is not just a chance meeting. When two souls recognize each other, life itself is transformed.You may feel her energy even before you meet her. The air around you becomes thicker, your heartbeat quickens, and that figure appears in your dreams, familiar and mysterious at the same time. Your connection needs no words, there is a silent understanding, an attraction that goes beyond physical appearance, beyond logic.

Twin flames are not simply lovers or friends. They are two halves of the same fire, separated by an ancient time, but destined to find each other. When your soul meets hers, everything changes: the colors are more vivid, the sounds more intense, and even the greatest challenges seem surmountable, as if you have found that hidden strength you've been missing.But their union is not always easy. It is a deep bond, capable of unsettling you, of making you question everything. You may feel the tension building up, like a storm that precedes the quiet. However, this bond does not break. No matter how hard you try, no matter how far you or the other person may stray, you will always come back to each other, because it is not just earthly love. It is something more, something sacred. The roots of this concept go back to ancient times, to when souls were united, perfectly balanced. But as time and lives have passed, they have been separated, forced to wander until they find each other again. And when they do, the recognition is immediate, as if the invisible thread that bound you had always been there, waiting to be reknit.

The history of the twin flame theory

There was a time, long ago, when human beings were not as we know them today. They were powerful creatures, with four arms, four legs, and two faces that looked in opposite directions. They walked the earth as giants, united in a perfect form, male and female, and in beings that encompassed both. They were one, complete, and their strength made even the gods tremble.

The gods, watching from above, began to fear the power of these creatures. They felt a force growing within them that could challenge them, threatening their kingdom. So Zeus, with his cunning mind, made a cruel but necessary decision: he cut these creatures in half, separating them forever. He divided what was one into two parts, leaving them to wander the world, incomplete, searching for their missing half.

The separation was devastating. The broken souls found themselves weak, without purpose. The sense of loss, the deep emptiness, became part of their existence. The sky seemed less vast, the earth colder. There was no longer that spark that gave them energy. But the gods, despite their thirst for control, understood that something had to be done. Apollo, the god of light and healing, proposed a solution: he would sew up the wounds leaving a visible mark, the navel, as a memory of what had been. A silent mark that reminded every being that its other half still existed, somewhere in the world.

From that moment on, every human being came into the world with an innate desire: to seek his or her lost half. It is not just a need for love, Wayfarer. It is something deeper. It is the thirst for wholeness, for finding that part of you that you feel is missing. And you, like all souls walking this earth, carry within you that burning fire, that silent but constant awareness that somewhere, someone is looking for you.

But the path to your twin flame is not easy. The gods, while recognizing the importance of this quest, have made it difficult, almost impossible. To meet your twin flame is to awaken an ancient power, a force that could rival that of the gods themselves.

That's why not all souls are found immediately. There are trials to overcome, lessons to learn. Every obstacle, every pain you feel, prepares you for that encounter, makes you stronger, more aware.

When you find your twin flame, wayfarer, it will not just be a meeting of two bodies. It will be an awakening.

Every fiber of your being will vibrate. The world around you will seem to change: the air will become denser, every color more vivid, every sound deeper.

Your trembling hands will touch his, and in that instant you will know that you have finally come home.

Twin flames archetype

Seeker, I ask you to pause for a moment. Listen to the beating of your heart, that deep echo that resonates within you, as if it were searching for something or someone you have not yet found. It is an ancient search, a connection that goes back to ancient times, when the world was inhabited by gods and goddesses, and the fate of souls was intertwined with that of immortals.

Aphrodite, goddess of love and beauty, and Ares, god of war, represent the power of twin flames. Two opposing, seemingly irreconcilable forces. She, the embodiment of sweetness, of passion that caresses all things, and he, pure force, destruction, chaos. They should have repelled each other, yet they sought each other out, like two magnets attracted by an invisible force greater than themselves.

Aphrodite, married to Hephaestus, the god of fire and forges, spent her nights alone, ignored and frustrated, while he was lost in the dull clatter of the hammer on the anvil. In this emptiness, Ares would join her. And when their hands touched, under the soft light of the moon, the world around seemed to stop. Each meeting between them was an explosion of energy that united them in an embrace that neither the gods nor fate could break.

When Helios, the eternal sun, discovered them, the gods were enraged. It was forbidden for them to love each other. Yet not even divine separation could keep them apart. They continued to meet, defying the order of things, and from their union seven children were born, including Eros, the god of love and desire, a reminder that when twin flames come together, they create something eternal, something magical, that no one can destroy.

Seeker, perhaps you, too, have felt that attraction, that force that pulls you toward someone, a bond so deep that it defies earthly logic. Some people think the twin flame has to be a lover, but that is not always the case. Your twin flame might manifest as a friend, a mentor, even a student who comes into your life to teach you something fundamental. It appears when you least expect it, often at times of greatest need, when you feel your path is dark and you need guidance. Twin flame relationships are intense, overwhelming, capable of shocking you to the core. They are like fire: they warm, but they can also burn. It is rare for them to last a lifetime, because often their destructive force is so great that it cannot be contained. When separation comes, the pain is inevitable.

But every encounter, even a brief one, leaves an indelible mark. It changes you, transforms you, offers you the answers you were looking for, even if in ways you didn't anticipate.

Do you already have a twin flame near you ?

Have you ever felt that invisible thread that binds you to someone so deeply that it transcends space and time? Your soul mate, or twin flame, is not just a person who completes you. It is a connection that goes beyond words, a silent recognition that vibrates beneath the surface.

Here are some signs that may indicate that you have already met your twin flame:

1) Time ceases to exist. When you are together, the hours fly by like minutes, but there is never any hurry or anxiety. You spend hours talking, sharing, and at the end of the day, you wonder where the time went. Yet, the desire to see each other again does not run out. *Like two travelers on the same road, never tiring of each other's company.*

2) Constant déjà vu. There is a strange feeling when you talk. Your experiences seem to intertwine, as if you have always been headed toward each other. It is as if life itself is pulling you together. *Perhaps you have had the same dreams, visited the same places or experienced similar events without knowing it.*

3) A magnetic force attracts you. When you are close, you feel a current in the air, like an invisible crackling between your energies. This is not just physical attraction, but something deeper, an understanding that expresses itself through shared silences. **It is a spiritual connection as much as a physical one.**

4) Your strengths and weaknesses balance each other out. Where you are weak, he or she is strong. And vice versa. Together you are invincible, two parts that complement each other perfectly. *As if you were born to support and balance each* *other.* Together you form a team capable of meeting any challenge.

5) A common purpose binds you together. You are guided by the same values, the same dreams. *Perhaps you both desire to help others, grow spiritually or create something meaningful.* It is as if you are moved by the same inner fire.

6) Deep knowledge and acceptance. You know each other in detail, down to your most intimate imperfections. But there is no judgment, only acceptance. **There is no need to pretend, because you know you are accepted for who you are.**

7) Do not fear conflict. Even when you quarrel, there is never a fear that you will separate. You know that whatever the dispute, you will always find common ground. **There is an unshakable confidence that your bond is stronger than any disagreement.**

8) The connection spans multiple levels. You are lovers, but also friends, fellow travelers and guides for each other. *Sometimes, a word or a glance is enough to understand you.* It is as if you have lived a thousand lives together.

9) Eerie synchronicity. You will often discover coincidences in your past or current lives. Perhaps you were in the same place during an important event without realizing it, or shared similar experiences at different times. *As if your paths have always brushed against each other, waiting to intertwine.*

10) Grow together. Your bond does not limit you; it expands you. The more time you spend together, the more compassionate, empathetic you become, able to understand not only yourself but also the world around you. *Like two trees whose roots intertwine underground, growing toward the sky.*

Why we need a twin flame

It is not the lack of a twin flame that makes you incomplete. We are already complete souls, capable of loving, growing and shining on our own. But a relationship with your twin flame has the power to take you to another level of existence. **It is** a journey **toward spiritual evolution**, a path that teaches you to shed your ego, heal the deep wounds in your heart and discover your true potential.

The relationship with a twin flame has no single purpose. It can manifest in many forms: an overwhelming love, a shared project, an inspiring friendship. **It can lead you toward a harmonious and balanced union**. Sometimes, the bond is expressed through raising children, working together in important causes such as protecting nature or supporting each other in spiritual growth.

But often, **the signs that lead us to our twin flame can be clouded**. Outside influences-such as grief or a bad relationship-can cloud your ability to perceive that deep connection. Heavy emotions, which drain you and make you numb, can blind you to the presence of a twin flame. **You may be so immersed in grief or stuck in toxic situations that you don't notice the gift that is waiting for you.**

Whether you are looking for a new spiritual connection or exploring the relationships you already have, **it is important to pay attention to how the people around you make you feel.** *Perhaps someone you already know is part of your spiritual make-up, and you don't know it yet.*

TWIN SOULS VS. TWIN FLAMES

What are the differences between these types of relationships? You may have already heard about what a twin flame brings to a relationship, but have you ever wondered what a soul mate really represents?

What are soul mates

Soul mates are people who come into your life and deeply transform it, leaving an indelible mark. **They are not just chance encounters, but connections that seem written in the stars.** *There is a sense of familiarity, as if you have met before in a distant time, perhaps in a previous life.* These people reflect a part of you, showing you not only your strengths but also your weaknesses. Through them, you can see more clearly who you really are.

The difference between a soulmate and a twin flame is in the depth of the bond.
While you have only one twin flame, the other half of your soul, **soul mates are extensions of your spiritual being.** *You can meet many soul mates throughout your life, and each has a specific role to play in your path.* Some may come as lovers, others as friends who bring light and meaning to your existence.

Soul mates make life richer and more meaningful.
They are not just companions; they are catalysts that ignite new perspectives, opening doors you didn't even know existed. *Perhaps there is a friend who encouraged you to follow a hidden passion, or a partner who made you see the world in a different light.*

Even if sometimes they only stay for a short time, **their presence always leaves an indelible mark.**

A soulmate should never put pressure on a relationship. Describing someone as a soulmate can create expectations, but a true connection with a soulmate is natural and fluid. *It is like a river that flows effortlessly.* **Unlike relationships with a twin flame, which can be turbulent and charged with extreme emotions,** a relationship with a soul mate is intense, but in the most joyful sense. **It makes you feel at home, relaxed and secure.**

Soul mates can stay by your side for a lifetime, **being like a stable rock you can rely on,** or they can be the lightning bolt that shakes you, igniting a brilliant idea, only to fade away shortly thereafter. *Think of a person who, perhaps even for just a few moments, said something to you that changed the course of your life.*

The relationship with a soul mate is a delicate balance of giving and receiving. These people are here to help you step out of your comfort zone, pushing you to grow when you need to. *Perhaps they challenged you to take that leap you had always put off.* Soul mates are meant to teach you valuable lessons, grow your spiritual strength and expand your consciousness. **They don't just improve you as an individual; they prepare you for a higher path.**

During your lifetime, you will meet many soul mates. Each encounter will be significant, and each of these souls will bring with them a piece of wisdom that will help you evolve. However, this may not be the case for your twin flame. **Not everyone meets their twin flame in this life, and this should not sadden you.** *It does not need to happen to have a full and fulfilling life.* You are already complete as you are. **But should you be blessed with a connection with your twin flame, be**

prepared for an intense experience, full of love but also deep challenges.

Signs to recognize the people in your soul group

When you make contact with someone in your soul group, **the connection is instantaneous**. There is no need for words; it is as if your connection was established long before you met. **The energy between you vibrates in an almost physical way**, creating a resonance that shakes you from the inside out. *Perhaps, in an initial exchange of glances, you feel something beyond the visible.*

The people in your soul group may come from all corners of the world, with different backgrounds, cultures and even genders. **But what unites you is something much deeper.** *It doesn't matter what your outward differences are, because you share the same values and dreams.* **You believe in the same things, aspire to the same ideals.** It is an affinity that goes beyond logic.

To really benefit from these connections, you must be open and receptive.
If you are blocked by negative thoughts, or if fears keep you from letting go, you may miss the opportunity to recognize someone in your soul group. *Negative emotions can make you put up walls that prevent light from coming in.* **But if you open your heart, every encounter will be a lesson, a growth.**

Where do you meet your soul group?
This is not an easy question, and often the answers you receive may seem vague. **There is no specific place, because these meetings happen when you are ready.** *It is like a door that opens at the right time.* That doesn't mean you have to wait passively; **opportunities come when you start looking.** Perhaps through new experiences, interests or hobbies.

Start by listening to what your heart is telling you. **The heart knows when it is time to step out of your comfort zone.** *Maybe there is an opportunity that scares you, but you feel you must seize it.* **Follow that visceral feeling, trust yourself.**

The Internet may seem an unusual place to find spiritual connections, but don't underestimate it. *Creating an online course or joining groups that share your interests may open unexpected doors.* Even if you don't find your soul mate right away, you are expanding your world and cultivating new connections. **Every step you take toward others is a step toward discovery.**

Signs that you have met someone from your soul group:

1. **Eye contact is intense.**
   When your eyes meet his, *you* **feel a deep and familiar connection,** *as if you have already shared something in another time.* There is no awkwardness, only comfort.

2. **Conversations go beyond appearance.**
   They will not be interested in how much you earn or your social status. **Their words dig deep, focusing on spiritual issues.** *Perhaps you start talking about global change, ecology, conscious living.* You feel that what really matters is your spiritual imprint.

3. **Attraction is magnetic.**
   Even if your time together is short, you feel a force drawing you toward them. **It is as if their energy envelops you.**

4. **You share the same beliefs.**
   Their words mirror your thoughts. **It is not just coincidence, it is synchronicity.**

5. **Time with them seems suspended.**
   When you are together, **time dissolves.** *Hours pass like*

minutes. You are so caught up in the moment that nothing else matters.

6. **They appear at the right time.**
   No matter if you don't realize it, **they will know when you are ready to meet them.** And they will often come at a time when you need support most.

7. **They challenge you without judging you.**
   Your soul group is not just there to support you. **They will push you to grow, to overcome your fears,** but they will always do it with love. *They will be the wind behind your back, never the wall in front of you.*

8. **You feel energized after each meeting.**
   After spending time with them, **your soul feels nourished, like after a hearty and satisfying meal.** *You feel full of life, ready to face the world.*

9. **You can be yourself.**
   You never have to pretend with them. **They see and accept your true self, without judgment.** *With them, you can drop all masks.*

The 10 archetypes of soul mates

Your soul group includes many souls who accompany you along the path of life, each with a different role in your path of spiritual and personal growth. Let's find out together who can be part of your spiritual consciousness and common humanity.

1) Soul partners
Soul partners are the most common connections you can meet. **They are not just limited to romantic or marital ties,** but can include life partnerships, such as close friends or colleagues with whom you share an important mission. *Think of that brother or sister with whom you have such a strong bond that it feels like a life partner.* These people accompany you through difficult times, support you and remind you how connected we all are in our humanity.

2) Reincarnated soul mates.
When you meet a reincarnated soul, **you may immediately feel an unexplained familiarity.** It is possible that you have lived together in previous lives and that there are unresolved issues to be healed in this life. *Perhaps you feel a strange tension between the two of you, something unspoken that seems rooted in the distant past.* It is important to look beyond residual feelings and judge the person for who he or she is today, to allow both souls to heal.

3) Romantic soul mates.
These souls come into your life to grow you through romance, but **they are not always meant to stay.** *They may bring immense joys or deep wounds,* but each relationship has a purpose: to teach you how to create lasting bonds and cope with life's difficulties. *A lover may constantly challenge you, but he shows you how to become a better person, even if your paths are not destined to cross forever.*

4) Soulmates.

Not all soul mates are romantic. **Many soul mates are those who make up your circle of support.** *Those few trusted friends who are there for you in difficult times.* They are the balm for your soul, the people you can count on for sincere advice or a word of comfort. **These soulmates are the spiritual nourishment you need to face life's journey.**

5) Soul families.

These people are not part of your biological family, but **they share your same passion and dedication.** *They might be members of a spiritual group or a community committed to a common cause.* Although you may never meet in person, the bond you share is deep, based on a mutual commitment to a common goal. **They are your spiritual family, united by the same vision for the world.**

6) Kindred spirits

These bonds are formed by sharing similar experiences. **They are not always kindred spirits, but their contributions are significant.** *You may be a young mother who turns to other mothers in the same situation for support, or perhaps you are a professional who finds comfort in those who understand the challenges of your career.* These connections bring understanding and support in unique ways.

7) Soul contracts.

These are not part of your soul group, but they are promises you make to yourself. **You have made a commitment to your soul to accomplish something important in this life.** *It could be a goal you feel you must achieve, a personal mission, or a significant change.* This contract gives you strength and direction, helping you persevere when the challenges get tough.

8) Soul teachers

These are the members of your soul group who **come into your**

life to teach you profound lessons. *They may be professors, mentors, or even people you meet casually, but they guide you in a way that changes the course of your life.* These teachers impart to you not only knowledge but also wisdom, opening up new avenues you would never have considered.

9) Soul crossings.

Sometimes, the briefest encounters can have an equally profound impact. **Soul crossings are like ships that pass in the night,** leaving an indelible mark. *It could be a lover you meet on vacation, or a person who touches you deeply but then disappears from your life.* These encounters remind you that **time is not the crucial element,** but what you learn and feel in the short term can be of great value.

10) Karmic soul mates.

Karma is not a simple punishment or reward, **but a system of growth and evolution.** *Karmic soul mates enter your life to help you correct your path or recognize your mistakes.* They may appear at key moments, bringing with them difficult lessons or great enlightenments. **They are here to help you evolve and align with your destiny.**

Your soul group is the support that guides you through life. Every soul you meet, whether brief or lasting, **brings with it a lesson or a gift.** And although you may never meet your twin flame, **remember that you are already complete as you are.** The people who cross your path are part of your journey of growth and evolution, and their job is to enrich your soul and help you discover who you really are.

SOULMATES AS LIFE PARTNERS

When you think of love relationships, the image of two people meeting, falling in love, building a family, and then growing old together probably comes to mind. **This is the idea of the "life partner,"** a person who stays by your side through thick and thin, sharing life's journey. *Two souls walking hand in hand toward a common future.*

But, what if it is a twin flame? **Is it ideal that your twin flame is also your life partner?** In most cases, the answer is no. **Twin flames are not meant for a peaceful and stable life.** They are two halves of the same soul, connected by an overwhelming, turbulent passion that can ignite the deepest and most complex emotions. *You cannot choose your twin flame; you are united on a spiritual level beyond human control.*

When you meet your twin flame, you will know, because the energy between you will be intense, like an approaching storm. **Twin flames will push you to look inside, to explore parts of yourself you may never have wanted to see.** *They will make you question everything, taking you from the peaks of ecstasy to the depths of darkness.* It is a relationship that cannot be ignored or taken lightly, because it will transform you, for better or worse.

The passion you feel for your twin flame will not always be sexual in nature, but **it will be so strong that you will feel you cannot live without them.** *Like an addict, you will feel the need for that connection, even if it consumes you.* People around you may try to warn *you, telling you to back off, not to hurt yourself.* But the bond will be stronger than any advice, because it is a call of the soul.

On the other hand, **soul mates are** also **destined to enter your life,** but with a different purpose. Soul mates are **deep, predestined connections.** *Perhaps you have lived together in past lives, shared experiences that now guide you to each other.* But soulmate relationships are not always permanent. *They may come to stay or they may fade away when their task has been accomplished.*

The difference between a twin flame, a soul mate and a life partner lies in their purpose. **All the relationships you experience before you meet your life partner serve to teach you something essential.** *Every hurt, every suffering, every joy experienced is part of your journey of growth.* They prepare you to recognize what you really need in a life partner.

When you accept love into your life, you are not just opening your heart to a person.

You are embracing the possibility of having **a plethora of deep, authentic connections** that make you more whole and help you build solid relationships that can keep you grounded. *It is a path that leads you to true stability, the inner security that comes from having the right person next to you.*

Types of relationships you should experience in your life

1) The Partner

A life partner is the companion you choose to share your love and journey together. **It can be your boyfriend, girlfriend, husband or wife.** *The definition of "partner" has no limits: it transcends gender, sexuality or traditional roles.* **What we all seek is a safe haven,** a place to retreat to when the world gets too heavy. *A person who is there for you in difficult times, ready to protect and support you.*

Traditionally, the male partner was seen as the "hero," the one who protected and saved his woman. **But today women take on equally strong roles,** ready to support and protect their partner with the same energy. *However, it does not mean that the heroic instinct should be ignored: it is part of male nature.* Let your man feel like a hero, *even in the little things: make him feel that he is important and necessary in your life.*

2) The Mentor

on all life partnerships are based on romance. **A mentor is a figure who guides and inspires you along your path.** *Perhaps it was a teacher who shaped your life, or a colleague who taught you more than you thought.* **Mentors are the people who help you grow,** both personally and professionally. *They offer you advice and practical support, without asking for anything in return.*

Some mentors stay in your life for years, **while others may come and go quickly,** but **their impact remains profound.** Even if they are no longer part of your daily life, you can still turn to them in times of need. *They are still there, ready to give you advice or a wise word when you need it.*

3) The Anchor

Who is that person you turn to when everything seems to fall apart? **The anchor is the partner who helps keep you stable in difficult times.** *It is that person you trust, who helps you see things clearly, even when life seems confusing.* **He doesn't just tell you what you want to hear,** but challenges you to consider all sides of the situation. *The anchor guides you, makes you think, and helps you set achievable priorities in your life.*

Anchors are not just emotional supports. *They can make you see things you can't see on your own, giving you different perspectives and helping you make more informed decisions.*

4) The Confidant

The confidant is the partner with whom you can be totally yourself, without filters or masks. *With him or her, you can share your deepest thoughts, your fears, and your darkest secrets.* **You know that your every word is safe,** and there is no judgment. *He or she is the person who understands you even when you say things that might seem exaggerated to anyone else.* With your confidant, you can speak freely and know that whatever you say will be listened to with care and understanding.

Having someone to vent to is crucial. *This kind of connection allows you to free yourself from everyday tensions, express your thoughts without fear, and feel accepted as you are.*

The 27 points of the life partner

1) A strong sense of self and goals:
 A life partner must be a complete person who is aware of who they are and what they want. **A person who knows where he or she is going can be a solid partner.** *You do not want a partner who depends on you to define his or her own identity, because you would end up carrying the entire weight of the relationship on your shoulders.*

2) Honesty:
Trust is the foundation of every relationship. *Little white lies, such as a polite comment about a haircut, are part of life, but when a partner starts lying about important issues, trust breaks down.* Without trust, the relationship quickly weakens.

3) Joy:
You should feel joy in seeing your partner. *If his presence does not fill you with warmth or happiness, he may not be the right person for you.* The company of a life partner should bring light to the darkest moments.

4) Sharing moral values:
Having a shared vision of morality is crucial. **Do not compromise on your principles.** *Although you may accept small differences of opinion, similar values create a solid foundation on which to build your life together.*

5) Accountability:
A life partner must be accountable, not only for himself or herself, but also for you and your relationship. **Being present, supporting you in difficult times, is what defines a life partner.**

6) Shared sense of humor:
Laughing together is essential. *A partner with whom you can share moments of levity will be a source of strength in difficult times.* Life is

full of challenges, and having someone who knows how to make you smile makes it easier.

7) Inner strength:
In times of vulnerability, you need someone who can support you. **Whether physical or emotional strength, your partner needs to be able to make you feel protected.** *Sometimes simply knowing that he or she is there beside you is enough.*

8) Ability to trust:
Mutual trust is the basis for a balanced relationship. **You need to know that your partner can trust you as much as you trust him.**

9) Maturity:
Being on the same emotional level is essential. *Immaturity in a love relationship will only lead to frustration and problems.* Both of you must be adults, able to handle difficulties and changes with responsibility.

10) Compatibility:
Compatibility should be evident from the first meeting. *If you fight over the simplest things, chances are that the relationship will not last.* You cannot force compatibility; it must be natural.

11) Independence:
A healthy relationship requires both partners to maintain their independence. *Having personal interests and space strengthens the bond rather than weakening it.*

12) Shared commitment:
Both of you must be ready to commit to the relationship. **Mutual commitment is what makes the couple grow.**

13) Vulnerability:
Being vulnerable is human, and a life partner must be able to show up without barriers. *An emotional wall will prevent you from really getting close.*

14) Debating skills:

Knowing how to argue is important. *A partner who knows how to resolve conflicts constructively will ensure that the relationship is not damaged by problems.*

15) Humility:

Humility is an essential quality. *An arrogant or self-centered partner will not be able to build a healthy and mutual relationship.*

16) Affection:

Make sure your partner has the same approach to affection as you do. *If you desire physical affection and he does not, there will inevitably be an emotional disconnect.*

17) Empathy:

The ability to understand and comfort is crucial. *Even if your partner does not fully understand what you are experiencing, he or she must be able to show you empathy.*

18) Balanced ambition:

There must be a balance in ambition. *If one of you wants a quiet life and the other aims to dominate the world, there will inevitably be conflict.*

19) Attitude toward relationships:

Having a healthy attitude toward relationships is crucial. *A partner who has difficulty building stable bonds may not be the right person for a long-term relationship.*

20) Open-mindedness:

Flexibility and openness to new ideas are vital. *An overly rigid partner will stifle the couple's growth.*

21) Loyalty:

Loyalty is a cornerstone in a loving relationship. *Without loyalty, there can be no trust.*

22) Mutual sexual attraction:
Physical attraction is an integral part of a loving relationship. *There must be a mutual spark that fuels the passion between you.*

23) Curiosity:
A curious nature enriches the life of a couple. *A partner who is open to adventure and new experiences will keep the relationship alive and interesting.*

24) Flexibility:
Being flexible is crucial. *Life is full of surprises, and a flexible partner can adapt to unexpected situations.*

25) Forgiveness:
No one is perfect, and the ability to forgive is essential. *A partner who holds grudges will only build up tension.*

26) Ability to enjoy the little things:
Life is made up of small moments. *A partner who can appreciate simplicity, such as a walk at sunset or a quiet dinner, will bring serenity into your life.*

27) Communication:
Communication is the key to all relationships. *A partner who can express himself clearly, listen and dialogue with you will be able to build a strong and lasting connection.*

THE RESEARCH PHASE

When you are searching for something deep and meaningful, like your twin flame, the quest can become all-encompassing. **You become completely immersed, like when you're looking for the perfect house.** *You spend hours checking listings, visiting neighborhoods, scanning every nook and cranny for the sign that will lead you to your destination.* Your mind is focused on that desire, and in that moment, everything else becomes secondary. But, **looking for your twin flame is much more complex.** You are not looking for a physical object or thing. **You are looking for a part of yourself, a spiritual connection that has been separated from you for millennia.**

This research may seem almost impossible, and for many it may seem like a waste of time. But stop for a moment. **Is it worth the search?** *Think about the possibility of experiencing a connection beyond the physical world, a spark that lights the fire of your soul.* The twin flame represents **the most intense and fulfilling experience you could ever have,** where every emotion is amplified, where the soul is fully awakened.

The concept of Divine Timing

Before diving into this quest, it is essential to understand **divine timing,** a concept that governs the journey of twin flames. **Divine timing does not follow the rules of the physical world to which we are accustomed.** *In the material world, we have been taught that we must work hard, strive hard, and only then will we get what we want.* But **in the spiritual world, control is not in our**

hands. You have to let go of the need for control and accept that **the universe has its own time.**

Changes in thinking:

1. **Abandon your ego:** *The ego tells us that we must control everything, that we must bend the world to our will.* **But on a spiritual path, you must become part of something greater.** Let the universe take control and guide your journey.

2. **Recognize that you have no power over the universe:** *Your willpower can change many things in the physical world, but in the spiritual world there is a higher force guiding the journey.* **Your path to the twin flame has already been charted, and no human effort can change that fact.**

3. **Reevaluate the concept of "surrender:" Surrendering does not mean weakness,** *but accepting that there are greater forces at play.* Open yourself to the faith and belief that the universe has a wonderful life in store for you, if only you embrace this truth.

From an early age, we have been taught the concept of "if you do this, then you will get that." *Tidy up your room and you can go play. Eat all the vegetables and you get dessert.* This conditional mechanism is also reflected in our view of the search for a twin flame. **We often think that we have to "adjust" to be ready for union. But divine timing does not work that way.** It is not a reward for perfect behavior.

Changes in thinking:

1. **Accept the positivity of divine timing:** *There is no punishment in divine timing.* **Whatever happens in your journey, you are exactly where you are supposed to be.**

2. **Recognize your progress:** Even when the path seems stationary, **you are always moving forward.** *Each step, each experience, brings you closer to your spiritual goal.*

3. **Trust the universe:** *Know that everything that happens is for your good, even if it seems difficult at the time.* **The physical world may seem like an obstacle, but on the spiritual plane you are always supported.**

There is no vengeful force ready to punish you for your mistakes. *If you have grown up with the idea that there is a higher power just waiting to judge you, it is time to let it go.* **Divine timing is not an external force that rules you strictly, but a part of you.** *There is a part of your soul that resides in the spiritual realm, an extended part of yourself that works with the universe.*

Changes in thinking:

1. **Recognize your connection to the spiritual realm:** *Although a part of you lives in this physical world, a larger part of you exists in the spiritual realm.* **This part of your soul is your guide,** *supporting you and pushing you toward greatness.*

2. **Rely on this extended part of yourself:** *When you let your spiritual self take control, things become much easier.* **Know the suggestions coming to you from your spiritual self,** and let them guide you along the way.

The journey to your twin flame is not just a physical journey.

It is a dance between the material and spiritual worlds, where **divine timing** plays the main role.

It is not a matter of effort, but of surrendering to the inevitability of the flow of the universe. Let go of the need for control, trust your higher self, and you will be guided to your intended destination.

How to prepare yourself for your twin flame

Now that you understand how the spiritual world is ready to guide you on your quest, it is time to prepare your body and mind for this journey as well. **Becoming the best version of yourself** means being ready, both physically and mentally, to face the emotional and inner challenges that meeting your twin flame can bring. This encounter could profoundly shake your balance, affecting your spiritual and physical health, so it is critical that you are in your best shape.

This path of personal growth is not something to be seen as a task to be completed. **It is an opportunity to discover who you really are**, inside and out, and prepare yourself to connect with the deepest part of your soul.

Start by creating a morning routine that helps you feel rested and energized. **The morning is when your energy is at its highest,** so take advantage of this natural momentum. You could start with a nutritious breakfast and a refreshing herbal tea, followed by some meditation or exercise. The morning is also an ideal time to make space, both physically and mentally. **Getting rid of some of the small clutter in your life, even if it's just clearing out a room, will make you feel lighter and more organized.**

Another important step is to **feed your mind**. The world is saturated with information, and although it may seem overwhelming at times, if you carefully filter what you receive, you can learn something new every day. Read books that stimulate your spiritual growth, try new experiences, such as a pottery class or a language lesson. *You may find that the universe is guiding you to something greater, perhaps the language of your twin* *flame!* The important thing is to be open to new possibilities and allow your mind to expand.

Physical activity plays a crucial role in your well-being. No matter what type of exercise you choose, **the important thing is to move your body**. *A 30-minute walk, yoga session or run can release valuable endorphins, making you more energetic and serene.* In addition to the physical benefits, you will feel stronger and more confident, ready to face challenges with a clear mind and a healthy body.

But don't forget to **talk to your spiritual self**. A part of you always resides in the spiritual plane, and this part knows everything. Take time to dialogue with this part of yourself. *Ask how it is, what it can teach you.* The universe communicates with us in many ways, often through signals and coincidences. If you are open to receiving, you will notice these connections everywhere. Maybe you'll find yourself chatting with someone who tells you about a perfect job opportunity for you, or who leads you in a direction you had never considered. **Synchronicity is the universe's way of guiding you.**

Another interesting step is to **write a letter to your twin flame**. Even if you haven't met her yet, you can begin to connect with her. **Writing helps you to focus on what you really want,** to formulate the questions you would ask this part of you. *What are your dreams? What are your fears? What do you wish for from the future?* In this way, you prepare your soul for the meeting, creating a deep connection even before you physically meet her.

Forgiving yourself is perhaps one of the most powerful acts you can perform. Looking back at the past can be painful, but **it is essential to let go of** the mistakes you have made. Perhaps you missed a job opportunity or made poor financial choices. Maybe you hurt someone or lost yourself in a relationship that was not good for you. **Forgive yourself for all these things,** because they are part of your evolution. Each mistake has taught you something and led you here, to this point in your journey.

Eliminating toxic elements from your life is the last but no less important step. **Toxic people and habits block you, weigh you down.** *Do you have someone in your life trying to control you, telling you how to live? Or maybe there are those who always seem to find a negative side to everything.* These people drain your energy and keep you from growing. **It is time to let go of those who do not support you,** those who try to bring you down, or those who compete with you in harmful ways. *You need to surround yourself with people who uplift you, who push you to be the best version of yourself.*

Preparing to meet your twin flame doesn't mean just waiting for it to arrive. **It means growing, evolving and becoming the person you are meant to be.** Only then will you truly be ready for the deepest and most powerful connection your soul can experience.

AWAKENİNG

The next phase of the journey to the twin flame is that of awakening, also known as longing. **It is an emotionally charged moment when you begin to feel a deep, almost tangible emptiness, as if a part of you is far away, separated.** This happens because the bond with your twin flame is unique: two halves of one soul traveling different paths, but destined to meet.However, your timing may be different. **While you are ready, have already embarked on the path of spiritual growth and feel the call of your flame, she may not yet be aware of the need to begin this journey.** She may still be immersed in her challenges, her life lessons, unaware of the spiritual connection that awaits her.

At this stage, desire sets in. **You sense an unresolved need, a lack that seems woven into your soul.** It is as if you know there is a part of you that is missing, a piece of a puzzle that you cannot find. *And so, you find yourself searching, exploring new ways to fill that void, trying to fill that spiritual lack with experiences, people or new interests.*But the truth is that none of these things can really fill that void. **That missing part is your twin flame.** Despite external searches, the desire remains, deep and pulsing. *It is like a constant whisper reminding you that there is something greater, a connection beyond the tangible.*

During this period, you may feel torn between reality and the spiritual pull. *Your daily life goes on, but underneath the surface you always feel that subtle tension, that unseen current pushing you toward something greater.* This is your soul's desire that is calling you to awaken your true essence, to prepare yourself for the moment when your two souls will meet and recognize each other.

It is not an easy stage, but it is crucial. **This is where you begin to deeply understand who you are, what you really want, and what parts of you still need to grow.** *This awareness is the fertile ground on which your connection with your twin flame will flourish.*

The wait may seem long and difficult, but it is during this time that you really prepare yourself to receive that love that is so intense and transformative. **Longing teaches you to trust the time of the universe, to let go of the anxiety to control everything, and to flow with the spiritual journey that has been written for you.**

Do you use relationships to fill your spiritual void?

Sometimes we believe that the more experience we accumulate in love relationships, the more ready we will be for that special connection. But the truth is that nothing, no previous history, can really prepare you for the **avalanche of emotions** that will overwhelm you when you meet your twin flame.

Immersing yourself in relationships that do not enrich you may in fact make you feel less ready. **You are ready to experience unconditional love only when you free yourself from the burden of past relationships.** This requires an open heart and a light spirit. And it is not easy if you are still stuck in toxic dynamics or in the pain of a love that is now over. It is human nature to seek companionship and comfort, but sometimes we risk getting stuck in the idea of "having to be in a relationship" rather than allowing true love to blossom naturally.

Perhaps you find yourself filling a spiritual void by constantly seeking a relationship. Do you find yourself feeling restless or dissatisfied when you are alone? This is a sign that you may be looking to external love for what you should be finding within yourself instead.

If you feel unhappy when you are single, chances are you are trying to fill a spiritual void with a relationship. **Happiness should never depend on the presence of someone else in your life.** You are a complete person, and your fulfillment comes not from a partner, but from yourself. *Travel, explore by yourself places you have always wanted to see, enjoy the freedom to create your own adventures.* Discover the beauty of your own company and learn to embrace the silence that only you can offer yourself.

When your mood swings depending on your partner's mood, you are allowing someone else to have control over you. **True love is empathy, not emotional dependence.** If you feel responsible for your partner's happiness or can't be serene when he is down, you need to ask yourself whether your joy really comes from within or is conditioned from the outside. *Being happy for yourself, even when your partner is not, is a sign of spiritual independence.*

What if anxiety consumes you every time you are separated? This is an important signal. **Independence is essential in any healthy relationship.** *Every couple needs separate spaces, moments to themselves.* If your partner's absence leaves you restless or empty, then there is spiritual work to be done on yourself. You don't have to fill your life only through each other; you have to nourish your own soul, enjoy each other's company.

If you need constant validation from your partner, then you may be trying to fill a self-esteem gap. **Your worth does not depend on what others see in you, but on what you know yourself to be.** *You don't need constant compliments to know how wonderful you are. You need to feel it deep inside, to recognize your worth.*

When a relationship ends, it is natural to feel sadness. But **the end of a relationship does not mean the end of your world.** *If you've ever felt that everything fell apart when a love affair ended, then it's time to take hold of yourself again.* Don't look for a new love to plug your wounds, but focus on your spiritual healing. **Fall in love with yourself again.** Regain your balance and inner strength. True wholeness comes when you realize that you are whole already on your own. And when you are ready, the love you seek will come, not to fill a void, but to add light to your life.

The awakening of the twin flame

One of the most frustrating parts of the journey to your twin flame is the waiting. Both halves don't always awaken at the same time, and this can make you feel suspended, as if a key part of you is still hibernating. You may have been working on your spiritual growth for a long time, feeling ready for that magical encounter, while your twin may still be lost in earthly dynamics. **You, awakened, already feel the connection, but your twin may still be asleep.**

A feeling of emptiness, of longing, begins to arise. You know that you are missing something, or rather, someone. And this makes you feel suspended between two worlds: the material and the spiritual. **It is as if a part of your soul is in the middle, missing, and you try to fill this void in different ways.**

But as time passes, you may begin to sense the presence of your twin flame even without physical contact. This is where you create a kind of **love bubble**, a dimension in which your souls can talk to each other, recognize each other, even before you meet in real life. In this bubble, you can sense his emotions, his thoughts, and you are often surprised at how intensely this connection manifests itself.

This state of connection can lead to strange phenomena. You may find yourself saying or thinking things you would never say in person, words that seem harsh or unexpected. **Yet, these interactions are not random. They are part of the process in which your higher self tries to shake your twin, nudging it toward awakening.**

Frustration is normal. You wonder why you feel this connection so intensely and he does not. But you have to remember that **the timing of the universe is not our own.** The twin flame with the feminine energy often tends to awaken first, while the masculine energy may take longer. And so, while you are in tune with your spiritual mission, he may still be navigating the turbulent waters of daily life.

When the union is close, the universe begins to send you signals. Perhaps you notice an inner calm that was not there before. **You no longer feel the compulsive desire to search for something, because now you know that you are complete.** Your soul shines with inner light, your energy changes, and you find yourself facing life with a new serenity, as if everything is in its place.

You may also begin to see tangible changes in your life. Some people feel a call to change their home, city or even country. **It is the universe guiding you toward your twin.** An irrational but deeply rooted impulse urges you to move, to follow a path that only your soul can understand.

Or, you might feel a constant chill, a kind of electricity in the air. It's anticipation, a sense of excitement that you can't explain. **Every day you wake up with that feeling of something extraordinary about to happen.** It's like Christmas Eve, that trepidation you feel without knowing exactly what's coming.

Sometimes, however, the universe gives you stability. Everything in your life suddenly seems in perfect balance: work, relationships, finances. **When your life reaches this peak of harmony, it's a sign that you're ready for a meeting with your twin flame.** It is as if the universe is preparing you, putting every piece in place to allow you to receive your other half.

Some, paradoxically, stop longing for that encounter. **You feel so complete and at peace with yourself that the twin flame becomes a plus.** You don't need someone to make you feel whole. Yet it is precisely in this state of wholeness that you are closer than ever to union.

As the meeting approaches, you feel more creative, inspired. **The energy of the universe flows through you, pushing you to create, to write, to devote yourself to new projects.** This creative flow connects you even more to your humanity and opens spiritual channels to receive divine messages.

And then come the dreams. Vivid, real dreams in which you meet your twin flame. **You may not recognize her physically, but there is something in those dreams that tells you it is him.** The words you exchange, the hugs, the sense of familiarity-- everything is a sign that union is imminent. *Maybe he's telling you "I'm coming for you" or "trust in the universe."*

Keep track of these dreams. **They are fragments of a puzzle that will come together once you meet in reality.** And when it finally happens, you will find that, in some way, you already knew. Your dreams have prepared you, your heart is ready, and the journey that seemed endless finds its conclusion in the sweetest of beginnings.

THE MATURATION PHASE

All the signs were there. You could feel that subtle chill running through you, that inner light that seemed to shine brighter every day. And now, there it was. Your twin flame has entered your life. **The missing part of your being, the other half of your soul, is now here.** For so long you have imagined this moment, and yet, now that it is real, it seems almost impossible for you to believe it.

It is as if time has played with you, creating an infinite distance between the two of you, only to dissolve it in an instant. Now you ask yourself, **"What now?"**

Now the real journey begins. It's not just about recognizing the other, looking into each other's eyes and seeing reflected all that you are. **It is about facing the wave of emotions that sweeps over you, a whirlwind of intense and sometimes frightening feelings.** You have never experienced anything like it. The connection you have always felt on a spiritual level now manifests itself physically, and the intensity can leave you breathless.

Your twin flame will bring you face to face with parts of yourself that you may never have wanted to face. **The love you feel is deep, but it is not just sweetness.** There will be times when you feel like looking in the mirror and seeing your fears, your insecurities reflected in his eyes. *Every emotion, even the most* *uncomfortable ones, must be embraced.* You cannot run away from what you feel, because it is part of your path.

But this is only the beginning. Meeting your twin flame is destined to transform every aspect of your life. **You will never be the same, because together you are about to embark on a mission.** It is a journey that is not just about the two of you, but about the elevation of your soul and everything around you. This union is not just a romantic experience, it is an invitation to grow spiritually, to realize your highest purpose.

You will feel a change within yourself, a push to be a better version of yourself. **Your twin flame will make you grow, not only as a partner, but as an individual.** He or she will guide you to a new understanding of yourself, and the world you knew until then will seem bigger, brighter. Every moment spent with him or her will be a step toward greater awareness, but also toward new challenges.

The intense emotions you feel -- love, fear, joy, uncertainty -- are all parts of this process. **Don't run away from these feelings, embrace them.** *Every emotion has a purpose, every feeling is a key to your awakening.* It may seem scary, but it is also the most transformative experience you can have.

Now that your twin flame is here, your life will never be the same. **It is time to let go of all fears, embrace change and allow your soul to evolve.** The journey has just begun, and the destiny that awaits you is one of growth, discovery and unconditional love.

When you meet a twin flame for the first time.

The signs of meeting your twin flame are powerful, something that cannot go unnoticed. **It is as if the universe is speaking to you through that connection**, making you feel a familiar presence that you recognize on a deep level, as if you have already met her in your dreams, in your innermost thoughts. It will not always be a romantic connection; your twin flame may appear as a friend, a mentor, someone who shares the same struggles, the same strengths as you. **But the intensity of the connection will be unmistakable.** A glance will be enough to bring out emotions so powerful they will leave you speechless.

You will feel as if you have been brought together for a greater purpose, a common mission that goes beyond a simple human relationship. This can be overwhelming. The depth of love, the strength of the emotions you feel, is something new and destabilizing. **How can you manage such intensity and, at the same time, remain productive, maintaining a balance in your life?** In the first moments of this union, it is not uncommon to have a certain amount of chaos. Such a strong spiritual connection between the two of you can lead to moments of confusion, even drama, because it is difficult to figure out how to integrate this into your everyday life.

Twin flames are bonded on a higher plane, but they must learn to live on this earth. This means that as much as you may want everything to flow naturally, you will need to find a balance and adapt your bond to a more concrete reality. Earthly relationships need structure, and even if your union seems to transcend all convention, it will be crucial to figure out how to handle it in the real world. Your love, however lofty, requires to be rooted, to find a place in your daily life.

Part of the challenge will be to recognize how your connection differs from "normal" relationships. The twin flame relationship has several elements that require balance, care and awareness.

One of the first aspects to understand is **the emotional connection between you.** When the twin flames meet, something inside you opens up, as if the center of your heart is wide open and you can love more intensely and deeply than you ever imagined. Think of how a mother synchronizes her breathing and emotions with the heartbeat of her newborn baby. There is an exchange of energy between the two, a flow that allows the mother to sense the baby's needs, to feel what she feels.

With your twin flame, the bond is just as deep. You and your twin flame awaken in each other hidden parts, wounds from the past, desires never expressed. **It is as if it illuminates your shadow, that part of you that you have always kept hidden.** And through this very connection, you have the opportunity to explore and heal those aspects of you that need to be released.

This union is not only about passion, but also about healing. **Together, you will work to heal the wounds of the soul**, giving you support, understanding, the courage to open your heart even more. *It is a dance of love and vulnerability,* a spiritual collaboration that transforms you into more complete beings.

How to strengthen the mental connection

The bond between you and your twin flame is already strong, but often the intensity of this connection can bring fears and anxieties. You find yourself constantly thinking about what could go wrong, so much so that you risk losing sight of the opportunities for growth and positivity that your connection brings. **Meeting your twin flame awakens emotions you've never felt before**, and this can be overwhelming. But how can you strengthen this connection without getting crushed by emotions?

Just as in a traditional relationship, the initial period of your union is a precious time. It is a time to discover each other, to explore not only the spiritual bond between you, but also the more practical and earthly aspects of your life together. **You need to get to know your partner in every detail, in their deepest desires, dreams and passions that define them.** It is not enough to know that you are destined for great things; it is important to find out what they love, what makes them feel alive. Ask them what were the most joyful moments in their lives before you met. What books inspired them? What places do they love to visit? These are small details, but they build deep intimacy.

Another crucial aspect is **building trust.** Even if your connection is spiritually intense, trust is not taken for granted. You must be transparent with your twin flame, especially when your feelings are confused or hard to explain.

There will be times when you feel in turmoil precisely because of them. **But it is in these moments that communication becomes the key.** Don't hide what you feel; open up, allow vulnerability to be part of your relationship.

Twin flames also argue. The intensity of your connection can lead to conflict, and arguments can often seem more intense than you would in a normal relationship. Emotions get amplified, and you may feel the need to assert your position. But remember, every word you say carries weight. **Avoid personal attacks, avoid hurting those you love more than anything else.** When you argue, do so respectfully, knowing that you both carry deep wounds and parts of you that the other can easily hit.

First of all, always ask yourself, "Why are we fighting?"

Disagreements often arise from small misunderstandings, but they hide deeper issues. Don't let insignificant issues drag you down, but address the real roots of the conflict. When you feel emotions getting too strong, don't hesitate to take a break.

Step back for a moment, breathe and let your emotions subside. Come back to the conversation when you feel calmer so that both of you can speak clearly.

Respecting each other's boundaries is essential. Never use words that you know will leave scars, even though you may feel hurt or angry at the time. **Your twin flame knows you better than anyone else, and you also know his or her most vulnerable spots.** Avoid hitting where it hurts the most, because although you might win a momentary battle, the damage to your connection could be lasting.

At the end of any discussion, **always find a way to reconcile.**

This is the time when you extend the olive branch, make a joke, hold out your hand. Even in the most heated conflicts, there is always room for reconciliation. **Returning to the closeness that unites you is essential,** because it is not only the spiritual bond that makes you strong, but also the ability to weather storms together.

Remember, your twin flame is here to help you grow, to bring to light what is deepest within you.

Together, you can explore the parts of yourselves that you have always kept hidden, and through this journey you will find a mutual understanding that goes beyond any ordinary relationship.

How to fortify the physical bond

When you meet your twin flame, something inside you changes profoundly, in ways you never imagined. **Your soul awakens and connects to a powerful force**, known as Kundalini, which transforms not only your spirit but also your body. This encounter releases an energy that permeates you, an intense flow that makes you feel alive like never before. Suddenly, you may feel invaded by an irresistible urge to embrace life, to share your love with those around you. Everything seems brighter, more intense, and your heart is overflowing with emotion.

But this awakening also brings with it physical symptoms that can disorient you. Kundalini energy, in fact, is a flow of pure power that moves every part of you, and sometimes its effect is so strong that it causes confusion. **It is not a matter of "good" or "bad" energy, but simply a matter of force being released and running through your being.**

You may begin to feel a deep connection with the world and feel the boundaries of your ego dissolve. **You feel part of something bigger, immersed in deep peace and boundless love.** The small joys of life - like feeling the sun on your skin or listening to the wind rustle through the trees - suddenly become incredible, giving you pleasure beyond words. **Your soul opens up and everything seems to align perfectly with your path.** This is the awakening of light.

On the other hand, the energy can also bring with it dark feelings, as if you are going through an inner storm. You may feel the need to isolate yourself from the noise of the outside world, because the sounds seem too loud, the lights too bright. **Your body vibrates with a new energy, and sometimes its release may feel violent, as if you are in the grip of a tremor**

that you cannot control. During sleep, rest may be disturbed, and you may experience hallucinations that make you doubt what is real and what is not. **Your mind tries to adapt to this new level of awareness, but the path is not always linear.**It is natural to feel bewilderment or fear when faced with these feelings, but remember that you are not alone. **Your twin flame is going through the same process**, and together you can support each other. Some people report being immediately sexually attracted to their twin flame, while others speak of a loss of interest in physical intimacy. This may depend on the type of relationship you are destined to have. **Not all twin flames are meant for romantic union; some are here to guide you spiritually or to help you grow in ways you had not anticipated.**You may experience rarer symptoms, such as feeling completely exhausted for no apparent reason, as if your body needs time to adapt to this new energy. **Dreams of snakes, symbols of the awakening Kundalini within you, may visit you during the night,** and with them you may experience a kind of spiritual rebirth, leaving you fragile, like a newborn baby.**The energy running through your body and mind can also cause sudden cravings, like those of a pregnant woman, or intense orgasms without any physical contact.** Your body is a channel for this powerful force, and you may experience physical changes such as headaches, nausea, or digestive problems. **But these are simply signs of your spiritual awakening.**The moment of Kundalini energy release can be extraordinary, as long as you are prepared. **Take care of your body, calm your nervous system and be compassionate with yourself.** Now is the time to support each other, you and your twin flame, as you go through this storm of new sensations together. **This is a time of profound transformation**, and although it may seem overwhelming, remember that you are in this phase to grow together, discovering new parts of yourself and your bond.

How to immerse yourself to the fullest while maturing your honeymoon

Being twin flames does not exempt you from the common dynamics of a relationship, even in the most romantic moments like a "honeymoon." You could be lovers going on a trip together or two kindred souls taking a break from the daily chaos.

 Giving each other time away from the worries of everyday life allows you to breathe, regain balance and connect more deeply.A trip together does not have to be luxurious or far away. **You can create magical moments anywhere, even in the comfort of your own home.** Share what you love: a special movie, a freshly baked pizza, a glass of wine, etc. These are simple gestures, but full of meaning when you experience them with your twin flame. **The intensity of your bond makes every little experience an opportunity to bring you even closer.**

If you have the opportunity to travel, the world offers incredible places where you can explore together not only new lands, but also new parts of yourself.

A trip to a spiritual place might amplify your connection, bringing out ancient and deep energies, as if the world around you were a mirror of your inner journey.But you don't have to go far to find peace. Sometimes, a simple getaway in nature, perhaps a weekend camping trip, is enough to reconnect you. Away from city lights and the noise of modern life, you can listen to the beating of your hearts synchronizing with the rhythm of the earth.

Every breath becomes deeper, every glance more meaningful.The secret is in the quality of the time you spend together, not the place. Even in the most ordinary moments, your energy feeds off each other. **Just be present for each other,**

letting the outside world fade away for a few moments, and you will realize that the real magic is in your connection.

Whether on a distant beach or in your living room, **every moment shared with your twin flame becomes an experience of spiritual growth and pure love**.

THE EVIDENCE - THE CRISIS

When does the verification phase begin in a twin flame relationship? There is no single answer, because it all depends on the intensity of the bond and the level of interaction you have. If you live with your twin flame, you may find that you enter this phase very early, when emotions begin to clash. Conversely, if your connection is less constant, such as if you only see her in the work or social sphere, it may take years before the verification phase occurs.

But when it comes, you notice it. **Subtle changes in the dynamic begin to emerge, especially after the first real conflict.** Even in the healthiest relationships, disagreements are inevitable, but when it comes to twin flames, turbulence is of a different nature.

Their connection is not only rooted in three-dimensional reality, but is elevated to a higher plane, where every emotion is amplified, every contrast is deeper.

A simple disagreement can feel like an emotional storm, not because the relationship is weak, but because everything you feel is more intense. **Every word, every gesture, is charged with a depth beyond the simple here and now.** It is as if your souls are trying to communicate something bigger, something older. **And this intensity can be scary.** You can feel overwhelmed, wondering why the emotions are so strong, almost uncontrollable. But the truth is that twin flames are meant to experience everything in an amplified way: love, joy, fear, pain.

Each experience becomes an opportunity to grow, to face the parts of yourself you have been avoiding, to look inside yourself with new eyes.

In this journey, the verification phase is not just a time of difficulty. It is an opportunity to strengthen the bond, to learn how to navigate through deeper emotions, and to discover how to face challenges together as a team.

The connection between twin flames is not only based on attraction or affinity, but on mutual transformation. And this transformation does not happen without some shocks along the way.

When you face these storms, remember that they are part of the process, not an end. They are a sign that your relationship is evolving, growing and pushing you to become better versions of yourself, more in tune with your soul and that of your twin.

The causes of the crisis phase

When doubts begin to creep into your relationship with your twin flame, it is easy to open the door to negative emotions. At first, everything seems perfect, you experience the "honeymoon period," and you believe that nothing can dent the special bond you have. **Every day you discover new similarities, details that make you feel invincible together.** But then, inevitably, there comes a time when something goes wrong.

Why does a estrangement happen between two souls that seem so deeply connected?

Think about how you felt before you met your twin flame. **Were you completely comfortable with every aspect of yourself?** Probably not.

 Many of us struggle with self-esteem, with self-acceptance, and when we meet our mirror image, these insecurities do not disappear; on the contrary, they emerge forcefully. This is where conflicts arise, not because you are not made for each other, but because your twin flame reflects you, highlights everything you still don't accept about yourself.

It is much easier to love someone different from ourselves, because that other person does not force us to confront the parts of ourselves we would rather avoid. But loving someone who is your mirror requires facing every part of you, even the parts you have tried to hide.

In an intimate relationship with your twin flame, physical intimacy can trigger old wounds and traumas, bringing tensions and emotional turmoil. **Sex, in this context, becomes an emotional battleground where old hurts can resurface.** You wonder if you will be able to overcome all that emotional baggage you both bring into the relationship, and the risk is that these unhealed wounds can turn into the core of your bond.

Why is drama addictive?

When the body experiences intense emotional tension, the brain releases opiate-like chemicals. **This makes the drama almost irresistible, an emotional addiction that drags you deeper and deeper**.

The more intense the conflicts, the more the body craves for them, and you may find yourself unconsciously looking for situations that feed this tension, because that is where you feel the energy of the relationship.

In the case of twin flames, this is amplified. **If one of you is inclined to seek drama, the other is likely to be drawn into it as well, because your souls are connected.** You may relive old wounds, reopening scars that were never fully healed, and lose sight of the beauty of your bond.

Recognizing the signs of this spiral is key to breaking it. You may find yourself constantly talking about your relationship with anyone who will listen, seeking confirmation or answers.

Or, in your mind, you replay every conflict, every word said, letting the pain and frustration take control. **You find yourself questioning everything, not finding peace either within yourself or in the relationship.**

Another sign is the feeling that you have lost your identity. **You no longer see yourself as an individual, but only as part of a couple, as if you have become an extension of your twin flame.** Your individuality, your essence, seems to have dissolved in the union.

If you find yourself justifying relationship difficulties by comparing them to stories of other troubled twin flames, it could be a wake-up call. **You should not seek solace in other people's drama, but find ways to transform your path into something positive and enriching.**

And if you notice that you are constantly turning to spiritual experts or tarot cards to understand your relationship, perhaps it is time to stop and reflect. The key to your relationship is inside you, not outside.

Finally, if your friends and family seem tired of hearing about your relationship and you notice that other passions in your life have disappeared, then it is time to take back control.

Don't let your connection with your twin flame become the only thing that defines who you are.

How to get out of the crisis circle

When you feel that the vicious cycle of your relationship with your twin flame is taking over, the first step is to take a deep breath and step away, if only for a moment. **Removing yourself from the immediate situation can give you the clarity you need to reflect**. Find yourself in a quiet place, in the dark, and focus on the rhythm of your breathing. In that silence, repeat to yourself, **"It's time for a change, something has to change."**

When you are in the midst of a crisis, **you are charged with a dark energy that seems to take over your life**. The drama becomes like a deafening melody that never stops playing in your head, following you everywhere, even in your dreams. It is time to break this cycle. To do so, you must release the accumulated negative energy and make room for new light.

One of the most powerful ways to do this is to "cut the cord." Think about who, besides your twin, is negatively affecting your life. **Imagine them bound to you by a thin cord** and, gently, visualize cutting that cord, letting them go with a blessing of light and peace. Every time you go to sleep, mentally repeat this ritual, freeing yourself from the day's toxic connections.

Taking pen and paper and writing can be another valuable tool. **Write down all the negativity you feel around you and within you**, every thought that is holding you back. **Bring to light those thoughts that tell you you are not good enough for your twin flame**. These words, once put down on paper, lose their power, and you can let them go, like leaves carried away by the wind.

To regain your balance, create a sacred space, a refuge for your soul. **This space can be physical, such as a room in your home, or a corner in a park where you feel at peace**. If you cannot create a physical space, do it in your mind. Close your eyes and visualize a safe place, a hidden garden or a distant planet where you can regenerate.

Do not underestimate the power of weeping. **Crying cleanses the soul, washes away repressed pain**. If you feel the need to cry and can't let go, watch a moving movie, let the tears flow and release your energy.

Even a simple salt bath can work wonders. **Sea salt, such as Himalayan or Epsom salt, has the power to clear negative energies** from the body and aura. Soak in warm water and let the salt take away any heaviness, any tension that drags you down.

Another key step is to **free yourself from external attachments**. Avoid getting too involved in groups or forums about twin flames. Sure, it's helpful to share experiences, but sometimes, without realizing it, you may be bringing other people's dramas into your relationship. **Your connection is unique**, and solutions to your problems must come from the two of you.

Once you get rid of the negative energy, it is time to forgive. **Forgiving your twin, and asking him to do the same with you, is the way to start again with an open heart**. However, do it only when both of you are ready, when pain and drama are no longer masters of your relationship. Remember, your bond is sacred, and every unhealed wound hurts both of you, because after all, you are one soul divided into two bodies.

Finally, **replace your addiction to drama with something positive**. Drama, even when it is painful, can become like an old habit that is hard to give up. **Find something to fill that void**: a new hobby, exercise, cooking, or simply reading a good book. The key is to replace the negative energy with something that nourishes the body and soul.

These steps will not solve everything instantly, but **by practicing them every day, you will help your relationship grow and strengthen**.

Twin flames are meant to enlighten each other, but also to work on themselves. Your journey is special and deserves to be experienced with awareness, without drama taking over.

How non-romantic relationships with twin flame create conflict

When you connect with your twin flame, even in a nonromantic context, **turbulence is inevitable**. You might think that without intimacy or sex the tension that often accompanies romantic bonds is eliminated, but **the reality is quite different**. The connection between twin flames transcends any form of conventional human relationship. When you meet your twin flame, you find yourself experiencing a dimensional shift, in which your spiritual growth accelerates, leading you to a higher version of yourself. This change pushes you to see the world from a different perspective, and suddenly, everything that previously seemed normal to you can become foreign.

Connecting with your twin flame inevitably leads to an inner change that will affect every area of your life. You may lose long-standing friendships; those people who were once an integral part of your world begin to seem distant. It is not their fault, nor yours, but simply your energies are no longer aligned. **The high energy you now carry within you can make others feel uncomfortable**. It is as if you are walking in another dimension, and those who have not reached that spiritual level may feel excluded, as if they no longer belong in your world.

Even work may seem less suitable for you. **Your soul now craves more**, pushing you out of your comfort zone. What was previously acceptable becomes unsatisfying. Your twin flame is not the direct cause of this discomfort, but the catalyst that triggered the change within you. **It is like going from economy class to first class; once you try it, you never want to go back.** And with this new awareness, your career or life goals may take a turn.

Family relationships are not immune to these changes. Your family may not understand your new orientation, and this can create conflict. **When you connect with your twin flame, your focus shifts to a higher level**, while your family members may remain tied to their daily expectations and needs. **The family drama becomes overwhelming**, and the need to distance yourself to protect your spiritual energy becomes a necessity.

As your awareness expands, **you become intolerant of petty behavior**. Gossip, lies, and power dynamics that you once accepted or tolerated are now unbearable to you. **You realize that your soul can no longer handle such low vibrations**, and this may lead you to detach from people who were once part of your daily routine. Your twin flame could be seen as the cause of this change, but it is actually your spiritual growth path that is leading you to desire a more authentic and luminous life. Your transformation may also be reflected in your daily habits. **Stimulants such as alcohol, caffeine or sugar will no longer have the same effect on you**. Your body and mind will begin to reject what no longer serves your well-being. Instead of frequenting bars or clubs, you may find yourself more attracted to places of cultural or spiritual enrichment, such as museums or natural spaces, where your soul can be nourished and regenerated.

Finally, **you will begin to follow your soul instead of your ego**. The ego, which often governs our decisions and relationships in the three-dimensional world, loses its power as you begin to connect with the divine plane. **Abandoning ego control allows you to flow with the universe**, following a path that, while not always understood by those around you, is right for you. This may generate conflict with those who do not understand your change, but **know that you are following a higher calling**.

relationship with your twin flame will inevitably bring turbulence, but it is through these challenges that growth happens. Some people and situations will leave your life, but they will make room for something greater and more authentic. **This is the journey of the twin flame: transforming, uplifting and leading toward a higher love and awareness.**

THE PURSUIT

At this stage of your relationship with your twin flame, you may feel a deep exhaustion, as if all the emotional whirlwind and conflicts have drained your energy. The years of dreaming and longing for "the one" now seem far away, almost unattainable. **The days of euphoria, overwhelming attraction and that intoxicating love** seem overshadowed by the difficulties and anxiety of the crisis phase.

This is where your souls show themselves in all their different degrees of maturity. **One of you may feel overwhelmed by the intensity of** the bond and want to escape, while the other, more mature or aware of the path, becomes the pursuer. This dynamic between escape and pursuit is typical of twin flames, but **it does not always manifest in the same way**. Personalities, experiences and life circumstances profoundly affect the duration and intensity of this phase.

If you recognize yourself in the role of "pursuer," it is essential that you understand the signs that anticipate your partner's escape. **You will feel the detachment even before it happens physically**, in the unspoken words, in the silences that weigh more than conversations. The deep connection you shared may seem blurred, almost inaccessible, as if suddenly there were a veil between you. This distance may make you doubt, make you feel lost, but remember: **separation can be a necessary part of the journey**.

There should be no anger or resentment at this stage. **Sometimes, pausing is the only way to heal and grow as a couple**. Your twin flame may need space to process, to find herself in the midst of emotional chaos. And you, as teacher and student on this path, need to accept the role you now play. The pursuer is not the one who coerces or forces, but the one who keeps the flame alive with her loving presence, while respecting the other's need for detachment.

There is no mistake in separating momentarily, as this pause gives both of them a chance to grow and reflect. The pursuer, instead of blindly chasing, can learn to give space and trust to the process. **Your patience and understanding become a silent guide**, an invisible anchor that allows your twin flame to find its way, without pressure.

When the other moves away, **it is not the end, but a phase of transformation**.

Both of you are learning to balance your energies, to understand the importance of individuality even in such a sacred connection. Don't force anything, but let yourself be guided by the knowledge that, whatever the distance, the soul always rejoins its own reflection.

How to recognize if your twin flame is a runner

In a relationship with your twin flame, it is critical to understand that the goal is not necessarily a lifelong romantic connection. **The connection goes beyond physical love and earthly desires.** Often, the male soul may feel drawn to other experiences, other people, despite the depth of the bond with the female counterpart. This desire to separate, to explore, is part of their growth process. **There is no need to rationally understand why it happens.** Sometimes, the only explanation is that **the male soul seeks space to evolve.**

When your twin flame starts to run away, it is not always aware of the reason. It just feels that moving away is the only way to keep growing. **The bond they feel is no less strong than yours, but their ability to deal with intense emotions may be more fragile.**

It all starts when you, the pursuer, begin to doubt the connection. **You wonder if this is really the relationship you want**, and slowly you begin to distance yourself. The detachment is not always abrupt or immediate. Sometimes, the separation manifests itself in small gestures, behaviors that speak louder than words.

A first sign might be "ghosting." **Suddenly, without explanation, your twin disappears.** He doesn't answer your texts, he doesn't return your calls, and you start to wonder what happened. **It might seem like an emergency or a sudden crisis**, but then you realize that he has cut all ties, blocking you on social media and changing his number. This is their way of avoiding confrontation, of not addressing the intensity of the bond you share.

In other cases, your twin may leave you hanging, **keeping you poised between closeness and distance**. One day he makes you feel at the center of his world, the next day he treats you coldly. It's as if he wants to keep the door ajar but doesn't want to walk through it. It is not always a sexual issue, but more an emotional tension: **he confesses his innermost thoughts to you, and then retreats as if it were nothing.**

Another sign might be their involvement with people outside your circle. **They spend more and more time with others**, preferring the company of friends or colleagues, and you begin to sense a distance that wasn't there before. This is not personal, but their way of seeking an escape.

The level of engagement may also decrease. **Social barriers, such as age difference or existing relationships, may become insurmountable obstacles** for your twin. You are willing to fight against these conventions, but they may not have the same conviction. Societal pressures, the fear of leaving what they know, or the simple fear of going against the grain may push them away.

But how do you repair such a relationship? How do you rekindle the flame when everything seems to have died down?

The first step is to recognize that you both need healing. There have been wounds, there have been moments of misunderstanding, but that does not mean that all is lost. **The kind of love you feel is intense, almost overwhelming**, and it requires you both to address what has remained unresolved. **Sit down and put everything on the table**, without fear. Sometimes, the most difficult conversation is the one that opens the door to true healing.

Repairing the relationship requires sincerity, vulnerability and the willingness of both of you to look within. **Only then, as you**

both acknowledge your fears and desires, can you find your way back to shine together.

Emotional mirroring exercise

The mirroring exercise is a powerful tool that helps you look inside yourself, recognize your emotions and reflect what you feel in your relationship with your twin flame.

This is not only about the problems between you, but it is a journey toward a deeper understanding of yourself.

To begin, find a quiet place where no one will disturb you. **Sit down with a sheet of paper and a pen, and let your thoughts flow freely.** Start by writing down everything that is weighing on you. Don't look for complex sentences; use simple, direct words, such as "I'm frustrated because my twin flame ignores me when I need her" or "I feel angry when she pressures me to do things I don't want to do." Let each emotion find its place on paper, unfiltered. Now, take a moment and reread what you have written.

This is the time to turn the perspective upside down.

Rewrite each sentence as if it were talking about yourself. For example, "I am angry with myself because I ignore my needs when I should be taking care of myself" or "I feel frustrated because I pressure myself to do things I don't feel I want to do."

Is there any truth in these new phrases? Often, what we criticize in others reflects something unresolved within ourselves. Perhaps you feel driven to react in a certain way because you have inner wounds that still burn, wounds that only you can heal.

Close your eyes and **visualize your pain as if it were a physical part of you.** Picture him next to you, as a separate figure representing your suffering. **Ask it what it needs.**

What would make him feel lighter, more at peace? Treat him as you would someone you love: hug him, sit with him, listen to him until you feel the weight melt away. This exercise will guide you toward greater awareness of yourself and your relationship with your twin flame.

Mirroring helps you become aware of what stirs the waters of your heart, and prepares you for more peaceful and constructive conversations. **Whenever you feel an inner conflict or growing tension, return to this exercise**. Let it guide you toward understanding and healing.

Insight into the running phase

When you enter the **Runner/Chaser** phase in your relationship with your twin flame, everything seems to intensify. It is not a physical estrangement that you can touch, but it is as if the other half is slowly withdrawing from the intensity of the bond. In these moments, the distance is not always in the body, but in the soul. **The runaway twin does not always leave physically, but does so emotionally.**
You may notice that they seek distractions: **drugs, alcohol, stimulants.** The intensity of the connection can become so overwhelming that the only way out seems to be to stifle those deep emotions with artificial pleasures. When their soul tries to find a way out, their first move is to turn off the pure energy that binds you together.

Spending less time alone is another key sign. They begin to surround themselves with people, plan outings with friends, and become anxious if the crowd gets smaller. They may seem to need a break from the deep intimacy they feel when they are alone with you. If you feel comfortable, let them handle the pace. Forcing them might just push them further away. And then there is that restlessness that takes over when you are together. **The energy of the meeting is so powerful** that they can become irritable, stressed, even provoke small arguments to get away. They don't understand why something so good brings them to such high levels of anxiety. **Sudden mood swings, sharp silences, distances widening.**

But unlike ordinary relationships, you will not see signs of emotional or physical violence. **A true twin flame will not consciously cheat or hurt you.** If these toxic dynamics occur, then it is likely that you are not experiencing a genuine twin flame connection. What you must remember is that **running**

away is often the result of incomplete spiritual maturity. Your twin may not be ready to handle the depth of your connection and needs time to work on himself. In those moments, the wise thing to do is to let them go. **Give them your blessing, and let them leave with love, knowing that if the connection is true, they will return.** The **separation** phase is painful, but it is also a sacred space to reflect and grow. During this time, take a step back and ask yourself, "Is this really my twin flame, or is it part of my soul group?" This space allows you to evaluate if there is still something you need to learn together, or if it is time to let go, even temporarily, so you can both evolve.
What if they come back?
 Twin flames, in the end, always come back. Not always right away, but the connection you have is bound to resurface, sometimes more than once, in a cycle of separations and reunions. There is no need to physically chase; the return will happen when they are ready.

The key is patience, not panic. During this period, instead of despairing, focus on yourself. Raise your vibration, return to your center. Remember the desire phase, when you were doing everything you could to be the best version of yourself, ready for the encounter? Now is the time to regain that strength. **Did you neglect your growth while you were with your twin?** Now is the time to rekindle your inner fire. Take time to **express gratitude** for the time you spent together. Gratitude transforms negative energies into love. Visualize the love you feel for them, feel the bond that never really broke. Love is a powerful energy, and even if distant, your twin will feel your vibrations.

Forgive. If you carry anger or resentment within you, ask yourself: would you go back to someone who holds a grudge against you? **Forgiveness is the most powerful act of letting go of pain.** It does not mean forgetting, but releasing the burden from your heart. Above all, **live in the present.** Your life must not stop while you wait for their return. Fill yourself with things that bring you joy, that make you feel alive. **Rekindle the flame within you**, cultivate healthy relationships with those around you, and keep the channels of love and growth open.

The twin flame journey is profound and unpredictable, but it is also an opportunity to grow, love and discover yourself in ways you never imagined.

Closing relationships ?

If you find yourself wondering whether you should permanently end the relationship with your twin flame, you are probably going through a delicate time full of inner contradictions. **The intensity of a twin flame connection can be overwhelming**, and sometimes keeping this connection alive requires exhausting emotional labor. Even if the love is deep and the chemistry unique, it may be that your path together is meant for temporary duration.

If, however, you feel that you can overcome the tumultuous waves that have accompanied you, and you can get to a calmer shore together, **you may stay together forever**. However, not all twin flame relationships are made to last in this lifetime.

How to know if it is time to stop chasing or run away?

When you stop seeing your relationship as a safe haven, and **no longer feel your twin as "home,"** emotional trauma may have taken over. The bond, which once wrapped around you like a warm blanket, may now feel like a burden, a place of tension and uncertainty.

If your twin responds with coldness or contempt when you contact him, this is a strong signal. **Respect is crucial**: even in the most difficult times, a twin flame should never become an enemy. If respect has broken down, it may be time to consider ending it.

Then, there is that subtle but powerful feeling: **instinct**. If your gut tells you that the relationship has run its course, listen to it. You have trusted your intuition before, and it is probably the same instinct that brought you into this relationship. Don't ignore the wisdom that arises from within you.

Sometimes, the pain the relationship has left behind is so deep that the only way to truly heal is to **end the process**. Continuing to communicate may only reopen old wounds, preventing both of you from finding the peace and balance you seek. **Healing requires space.**

What can you take from this relationship with the twin flame?

First of all, recognize that **this connection is unique**. Even if you have separated, the bond with your twin flame does not completely dissolve. **You will continue to be a part of each other** no matter where life takes you. When such a deep relationship ends, it is natural to go through intense emotions: grief, anger, frustration. **Embrace these feelings, let them flow through you.**

Celebrate the positive moments you have experienced together. Those memories, those fragments of joy and deep connection, are pieces of a puzzle that contributed to your spiritual growth. Let go of the negative, let the past stay where it is. **Every lesson you learned brought you closer to transformation.**

Although this part of your story may have come to an end, **your soul's journey is not over.** You may meet again, in another time, in another dimension. Twin flames are destined to meet again and again, in ways that defy time and space.

THE SURRENDER PHASE

This stage of the twin flame journey is often called "the magic formula" or "the silver bullet" because it represents the moment when you have to completely let go of all control. **You reach a point where you realize that being powerless is, paradoxically, the most powerful way to live.** This is the moment when you realize that you cannot hold back what is not meant for you and, at the same time, you have to let go of what you think you want to own.

Let go of all attachments. Not only to people, but also to the ideas, expectations and illusions you have built around your twin flame. Sometimes, it is precisely what you cling to that keeps you from moving forward. You have to trust the universe, you have to believe that no matter what happens, your destiny has already been written.

People often fear that their relationship with their twin flame is ego-driven: that part of you that wants to be seen, that seeks validation, that wants to be in control. But **true love, the kind that rises above human barriers, cannot be shackled by ego**. **You have to surrender to the divine** and stop trying to control everything.

Think of your relationship as a rose. You have been willing to offer the petals, those beautiful, bright moments that made you feel connected. But you also clung to the thorns, the difficult moments, the pain and moral challenges. Why did you do that? Because the ego is what drives you not to let go. It makes you believe that if you cling to pain, you are protecting something precious. But in reality, **the true beauty of a rose lies in accepting both petals and thorns**, because together they form the complete flower.

Surrendering means opening your heart completely, allowing love to flow beyond the boundaries of the mind and conventions. The ego wants to define you, wants you to conform to what society says is right or wrong. But why should you allow these boundaries to govern your love? **Love between twin flames is a love that knows no boundaries, it does not abide by the rules of earthly logic.**

What if your twin flame is from a different culture? Or is in a different relationship? **The reality is that relationships end, they change, and people evolve**. If your flame is meant for you, it will come. No matter what the current circumstances are: **fate always has the final say.**

Surrender also means putting yourself first, not in a selfish way, but to recognize that only by taking care of yourself can you truly love the other person. **If you continue to sacrifice yourself for others, no one will benefit**. The courage to surrender is to refuse to live a life ruled by fear and limits. It is letting love flow freely, without being stifled by social expectations or personal insecurities.**Be ready to challenge the world.** Let destiny guide your path and stop worrying about the barriers society tries to put between you and your flame. **Your love is illogical, but sublime, and it is destined to overcome every obstacle.** There is nothing that can stop two souls that are meant to be together.

The universe always supports you. It will follow you until you have fully embraced your twin flame experience, until you are free and ready to embrace this love with every fiber of your being.

What to expect when you give up

When you let your ego take control, you think that inner peace will come only when everything is perfect around you. But **true peace comes when you learn to find it within yourself,** despite the external chaos. When you surrender to this process, you completely change your worldview. It is like turning reality upside down and embracing a new truth: **You are the balance point of your universe.**

On this journey, you will discover many hidden truths. You will begin to focus your energy on yourself, instead of obsessing about your relationship with your twin flame. This change in perspective will allow you to grow. **You will feel a sense of lightness,** because you will realize that every negative emotion you project is only coming back, amplified, and affecting yourself.

You cannot control your twin, his actions or thoughts. **The only thing you can control is the way you react.** This simple, but profound, teaching will change the way you deal with every situation. In the past, you may have confused the pain of toxic relationships with love, and looked for flaws even in your twin flame. Now, instead, **you will learn to appreciate what you have,** to be grateful for every moment you share, without looking for anything else.

You will feel a new serenity in solitude, because you will realize that you don't need anyone to complete you: you are already complete. Your conversations with your twin flame will become deeper, even on an astral level. You will be able to feel his presence even when physically distant, **as if you were together, wrapped in an invisible but real connection.**

You will begin to send love to your twin with a natural ease, expecting nothing in return, knowing that love is the most powerful energy. And when you slow down, when you allow the world to move on without trying to keep up, you will feel more grounded, more calm. Stress symptoms such as headaches or muscle tension will fade away.

The synchronicities you share with your twin will become a source of comfort. Instead of getting irritated by coincidences, you will begin to find a sense of security in them: you will know that he or she will always be part of your life in some way. When you feel this connection, you can send a telepathic thought, a mental caress, and wait for a response.

And then there is the meeting of science and spirituality. **You will find yourself fascinated by what unites the two worlds.** Crystals and stones will begin to have new meaning, and you will feel a call to spiritual places, such as retreats or sacred temples. At the same time, you may feel drawn to scientific readings that try to explain what until now seemed inexplicable.

Along this path, **you will be more sensitive to your twin's mood swings.** You will no longer see these ups and downs as a disturbance, but as a necessary part of your bond. **Your energies do not always have to be in perfect sync,** but it is important to face challenges together, even at a distance.

Over time, you will notice how much your ability to communicate telepathically has been refined. Every thought you send will be charged with positive energy, wrapped in white light. Visualizing how your message will be received will help you feel connected, **as if your twin can hear you wherever they are.**

You will come to **experience total love.** Without any more fear or judgment, you will be flooded with the deep love you feel for your twin, and you will realize how extraordinary your connection is. **Looking into his eyes, you will see the origin of your soul, the place from which everything began.** It will be like recognizing an ancient bond, a spiritual home to which you belong.

At this point, your attraction will also manifest on the physical plane. **If the universe sees fit, it will guide you toward a concrete reconciliation.** Follow the signs. An unexpected invitation or a sudden trip could be the key to bringing you together.

Finally, you will come to a surprising conclusion: **this relationship is the most complete one you will ever have,** and even if the separation lasts, that will not change its importance. **No matter if you never meet again in this life,** the love you share is eternal and transcends all earthly boundaries.

When you surrender to destiny, you discover a new life purpose. **You will no longer worry about what others think,** and you will find the courage to express your true self, including through clothes, styles and choices that reflect your authenticity. You will be guided by a new thirst for knowledge and embrace your inner child, finding joy in small things, like painting or running in a park.

You will no longer be a spectator, but a participant in life. And, once you let go, you will find that the universe has always supported you, helping you grow spiritually and prepare for your next great adventure.

102

REUNION OR UNION OF THE TWIN FLAME

The end of the journey with your twin flame is near, and this moment brings with it a sense of stillness and awareness. **It is not just the "happily ever after" you know from fairy tales, but a deeper stage** where you become one and the world accepts you for who you are as a couple. However, the road to this point is different for everyone.

Separation can take many forms. **Perhaps your twin has moved away physically, cutting all ties, or perhaps you still live together but have lost each other emotionally.** The void between you may be invisible to the eyes of others, but you feel it as a looming shadow. **Yet even in this distance, there is growth.**

You may feel stuck in a cycle of separation and reconciliation, like a wheel spinning nonstop. **Sometimes it's like living on a roller coaster: drama and fear alternate with moments of intense passion and love.** This happens when you and your twin are at different stages of your spiritual journey. **Not all hearts are ready at the same time,** and some couples struggle to achieve reunion because they are still anchored in the 3D world, unable to ascend.

But if this is your case, do not despair. **Your soul has many lives ahead of it,** and time is not an enemy. Even if you are not reunited in this life, the connection you share is eternal and will bring you together when you are both ready.

What is important to remember is that reunion does not follow a linear path. Each couple has its own pace, and each person's journey is unique. Some twins separate for years, not because they do not love each other, but because they have to resolve their inner wounds before they can meet again. **Life is complex, and it often carries emotional baggage that prevents us from fully committing.**

If you find yourself in this situation, where you feel that your twin has stretched a "dangling carrot" in front of you, leaving you in a state of uncertainty, it may be time to face reality. **You will know within yourself when it is time to take a step forward, to overcome the doubts that are holding you back.** And when that happens, you will accept that whatever the outcome, it will be guided by fate.

When the signs show up, listen to them. They will be as clear as a breeze gently nudging you in the right direction. Act with courage and confidence, knowing that what will happen will be exactly what needs to happen. **Fate has already written its plan,** and at that moment you will feel a deep peace of mind, knowing that you have made the right choice for your soul.

This is your journey, your journey. No matter how long it takes or how complicated it may seem. The reunion, or the acceptance of separation, will get you exactly where you need to be.

Signs that you are about to meet a meeting

The end of the journey with your twin flame is near. "Happily ever after" is not the end of a fairy tale, but a point of arrival where **you and your twin become one**, accepted not only by yourself but also by the world. Every separation is different. **Perhaps your twin has left all contact, or perhaps he still lives with you, but has drifted apart emotionally.** This can happen when both of you are at different levels of spiritual growth, and unfortunately some couples get stuck at this stage without being able to ascend.

But fear not, **the soul's journey does not end in one lifetime.** Even if you fail to achieve full union in this existence, **there will be other opportunities.** The final reunion is unique to each couple and may take years of separation to resolve deep wounds and emotional scars. The lives of twin flames are often complicated, and the emotional baggage of one or both halves may prevent full commitment.

However, there are signals the universe sends you to let you know that reunion is near. **You may have sensed that your twin is holding back, and may have adopted a wait-and-see attitude.** When you feel the time has come to overcome your uncertainties, **take action**. It may be the spark that will bring you back together, or perhaps it will lead to a different turn of events. **Either way, fate will take care of what needs to happen,** and you will feel at peace.

One of the first signs that union is near is an unexplained excitement. You suddenly feel lighter, with a quiver in your heart. This is your soul recognizing a change in your twin's energy. **You may have already accepted the bond, but now he too is opening to the union.**

Communication between the two of you may become more fluid. **Even if you have gone through periods of silence,** you may begin to receive signals, such as dreams or sudden messages on social media. Even if you are thousands of miles apart, **you are still close on the astral plane.**

If your twin was already involved in another relationship, **you may feel that his situation has changed.** This could be a sign that he is getting closer to you, but don't allow your life to hang in the balance while you wait. **You cannot interfere with your twin's free will.** Keep living, look for new opportunities for love and let the universe take its course.

The reflection principle is another key sign. If you suddenly find yourself thinking about your twin more than usual, **chances are he is also thinking about you.** Your change in thoughts reflects a change in his heart as well. Often, you may hear close people mentioning his name or see signs of his return. These little clues from the universe prepare you for his reappearance.

When you meditate, look for concrete answers. If you feel your twin is ready but have doubts, use meditation to ask for clarity. Focus on your thoughts and ask if reunion is near. **If the answers don't come, don't worry.** There may be obstacles still preventing the union, but everything has its time.

The universe will push you toward reconnection in unexpected ways. **You might feel drawn to a particular place or event, as if something is guiding you.** A bookstore, a coffee shop, or even a minor incident might connect you with someone who knows your twin. Every coincidence, every little sign, leads you toward him.

And finally, **inner peace is the most powerful sign.** When you realize that you no longer need to wait, when you feel complete on your own, **that is when union is most likely.** The need fades away and gives way to serenity. There is no more anxiety, only a deep sense of completion.

Perhaps, at that point, **you will feel like your twin is already with you.** You may begin to sense him next to you, to feel him in your home, in your daily life. This is a clear sign that you are spiritually ready for a reunion.

Creative awakening is another strong sign. If you find yourself writing, drawing, or immersing yourself in artistic activities, **your soul is preparing for union.** Your creativity is a reflection of the joy you feel in your heart, and what you create will be something to share with your twin when you are together.

Finally, pay attention to the numbers. **The universe often communicates through numbers,** whether they are on an account, a watch or a bill. If you notice repetition or significant numbers, **these are messages guiding you toward reconnection.**

Eventually, **when you completely surrender to the flow of destiny, you will feel reborn.** You will be at peace, knowing that everything that happens is for your highest good. And when you stop looking, your twin will return to you.

What happens once you are reunited ?

When the separation phase ends and you completely surrender to the union, **the reunion will happen naturally**. You cannot force it, you cannot control it. It happens when both of you are ready, when your souls have found the right balance. **At that moment, your minds begin to merge,** creating a shared awareness that goes beyond words. It is as if an invisible thread binds you together, allowing you to sense what the other feels, even from a distance.

Three important realizations emerge at this stage of your journey.

The first: understand the deeper meaning of your partnership. It is not just a romantic bond; it is much more than that. **You are both aware of your roles within the relationship,** but this awareness goes beyond stereotypes. Whether you are a traditional couple or not, what matters is that you are **completely comfortable in your being.** The female partner might take care of communication, cultivate dialogue, while the male partner takes care of protection and support. However, for you, the roles can be fluid, with no constraints. **What matters is harmony, sincerity,** and feeling free to be yourself without reservation.

The second: when you work together, you form an unbeatable team. In the past, you may have struggled to maintain your individual power, made difficult by the conflict between the need for independence and the fusion of togetherness.

 But now you have learned to trust each other, to see your strengths as complementary. **There is no longer competition, only a unified energy.** Together, you are an unstoppable force.

The difficulties you faced before have been lessons that now allow you to **work together seamlessly,** with no more resistance.

Finally: you are meant to be together. Perhaps, in the past, you needed space, felt pressure to protect your personal space, to have moments of solitude. But now, **your home is wherever you both are**.

Whether it is a big house or a small apartment, the important thing is to be together. **Place no longer matters,** because you have realized that it is the connection between you that makes each space the best place in the world. Deciding where to live is no longer a cause for conflict, **but a shared choice,** made with serenity and love.

Each step in this journey has prepared you to experience union in a deeper, more conscious and more complete way. **Now you are ready to share not just a physical space, but a spiritual experience.**

NUMEROLOGY AND TWIN FLAMES

Numerology plays a key role in the twin flame journey, as recurring numbers are signs of the universe that indicate important milestones on the spiritual path. These numbers never appear by chance, but carry profound messages related to your inner growth and connection with your twin flame.

111: Spiritual Awakening

When you encounter the number 111, the universe is urging you to **awaken your consciousness**. It is one of the most powerful numbers related to twin flames, a symbol of opening spiritual portals. This number guides you toward greater awareness of yourself and your connection to your twin flame. You may feel a strong attraction to your twin, as if your souls are beginning to recognize each other on a deeper plane. *Your heartbeat may synchronize with that of your flame without you realizing it.*

222: Harmony and Balance

The number 222 is a symbol of **balance and harmony**. When it appears, the universe is reminding you to maintain a positive outlook despite challenges. In a twin flame relationship, 222 invites you to cultivate patience and trust. The path may be difficult, but this number assures you that peace and unity are on the way. *It is the gentle sigh that reminds you to let go of anxiety and embrace harmony.*

333: Expansion and Growth

333 is the number of expansion. It encourages you to **follow your spiritual truth**. During the twin flame journey, this number

represents a step in the growth process. It means you are both expanding your awareness and preparing for a deeper union. This number also invites you to seek spiritual guidance or practice activities that elevate your spirit, such as meditation or journaling.

444: Protection and Stability

444 carries with it a message of **protection**. It indicates that spiritual energies are aligned to protect you and your twin flame along the way. If you feel lost or unsure, 444 reassures you that you are guided and protected by the universe. *It is like the gentle touch of an invisible hand guiding you through the chaos.*

555: Transformation

When you see 555, get ready for a great **transformation**. This number heralds major changes in your life and in your relationship with your twin flame. If you are in a phase of separation, 555 may signal that the time of separation is coming to an end and that you are both ready for a new phase together. *Like a butterfly breaking free from its cocoon, you are about to be reborn.*

666: Reconnecting with the Balance

Despite this number's bad reputation, 666 is inviting you to **reconnect with balance**. It is prompting you to look inward and release negative thoughts or emotions that are holding you back. In the context of twin flames, it may indicate that it is time to let go of old patterns that no longer serve you and reconcile with yourself.

777: Divine Enlightenment

777 represents **divine wisdom**. If you encounter this number, it means you are in tune with your spiritual path and are receiving messages from the universe. You may feel closer to your twin flame or notice greater clarity regarding your life purpose. *It is*

the sound of the cosmic symphony inviting you to dance with the universe.

888: Abundance and Union

888 is the number of **abundance** and fulfillment. It signals that the fruits of your spiritual work are about to manifest. In your relationship with your twin flame, 888 indicates that you are ready to experience a deeper and more fulfilling connection. This is a sign that union is near, and that the universe is supporting you in achieving your mission.

999: Completion of a Cycle

999 indicates the **end of a cycle**. This number is deeply transformative and announces that an important phase of your life is coming to an end. In the twin flame journey, it can signal that you are ready to let go of the past and enter a new phase in your relationship. *Like the sunset of a long day, the number 999 invites you to close with what no longer serves you, to make room for new possibilities.*

GUIDED EXERCISES

In this part of the book you will find a series of guided exercises to experience twin flames and help you evolve spiritually in your relationship consciousness.

The Research

(Root Chakra - Muladhara)

Visualization:
You walk barefoot on a dark, damp earth, each step sinking lightly into the soft soil. The air around is cool, the wind caresses your skin, and beneath you you feel something deeper: roots. Your roots, strong and powerful, extend from the center of your body, reach down into the depths of the earth, seeking nourishment, stability. With each breath, the roots reach out, penetrating the fertile soil, finding anchorage, as your body straightens, strong and secure. **You are part of this earth, firm and still.** Each step brings you closer to what you seek, to your twin flame, but first you must find your balance, your security.

The scent of wet earth fills your lungs, the sound of leaves moving above you reminds you that you are safe, protected by nature itself. **Each root is an invisible thread that connects you to your soul mate.**

Meditation:
Close your eyes and bring your attention to your root chakra. There, at the center of your base, pulses a red, warm, vibrant

light. **Can you feel it? It is a slowly growing flame, radiating strength, stability, power.** Breathe deeply and let that light expand, filling every corner of your body. Your spine is a column of energy, solid as a mountain, and each breath brings you one step closer to awareness. **You are supported by the universe on this journey.** There is no hurry, just a path to be walked with patience.

Each breath brings you back to the here and now. The red light becomes the very beat of your heart, slow, powerful. Feel it take root within you, an invisible link between you and the earth, between you and your soulmate, drawing closer with every step.

Associated stone:
Hold a hematite in your hand, cold and smooth. **Can you feel its weight? It is your shield, your protection.** It roots you, wraps you in silent security, and allows you to walk without fear. Keep it with you, at times when you feel the ground wavering under your feet, when the world seems to move too fast. *In those moments, hold the hematite in your hand and let its silent power envelop you.*

Associated Planet:
Saturn watches you from above, stern and patient. He doesn't rush, doesn't hurry. **It teaches you the lesson of time, of structure.** *Every difficulty, every delay, is a karmic lesson, a step toward your evolution.* Saturn invites you to endure, to remain solid, like a tree that has seen storms pass, never bending.

Motivational Shadow Work:
Face your deepest fears. Look into the face of loneliness and abandonment, don't look away. *The wound stings, but it is necessary.* Only by facing these shadows can you truly begin your journey. **The search is not a desperate act, but the first step toward your healing.** Rooted in self-sufficiency, feel the strength hidden within you, and realize that you don't need anyone else to make you feel whole. But the moment you are rooted, strong, you will be ready to meet the other. **You are your beginning.**

The Encounter

(Sacral Chakra - Svadhisthana)

Visualization:

You stand on a silent shore, where the water gently laps against the land, creating a gentle, steady rhythm. **The sound of the waves surrounds you, hypnotic, like a whisper calling you to let go.** In front of you, a figure emerges from the thin mist, and without words, you know it is him, your twin flame. Your eyes meet, and time seems to slow down. Water, a symbol of your deep emotions and sexual energy, moves between you, creating an invisible bond that grows with each breath.

The air is thick with anticipation, the salty scent of water fills your senses, and the touch of the waves on your skin reminds you how alive this connection is. **You feel the desire and strength of your union flowing like a raging river.** Every heartbeat is synchronized, every breath is a dance between two souls destined to find each other.

Meditation:

Close your eyes and bring your attention to your sacral chakra, just below the navel. An orange light emerges, warm and fluid, like slowly moving lava. **Feel the energy rise, stimulating your creativity, your passion, your vitality.** Let this light flow through your body, releasing every blockage, every fear. Every emotion you feel is pure, natural, opening you to the possibility of deep connection, without barriers. **Let go of your emotions, let them flow as freely as water.**

Each breath is like a rising and falling wave, fluid and natural. The orange light expands, warming every corner of your body, awakening your most authentic desire. Feel that inner flame grow, pulsing and alive, ready to connect with each other.

Associated stone:
Hold a small coral in your hand, smooth and warm. **Feel its power awaken your creativity and open your emotional expression.** *Whenever you feel stuck, squeeze the cornalina and let its energy guide you to emotional freedom.*

Associated planet:
Venus, bright and soft, watches from above. **She teaches you the beauty of love, of sensual connection, of pleasure.** *In its light, there is the promise of deep union, honoring every part of you.* **Do not be ashamed of your desires; they are part of your essence.**

Motivational Shadow Work:
Look deep inside yourself, there where you hide the most intense desires, the ones that scare you. **Let them rise to the surface, without judgment, without shame.** *What do you really desire? What are your most authentic needs?* Feel them, accept them, and give yourself the right to want them. **Only by accepting your hidden desires can you truly connect with each other.** Intimacy is not weakness; it is strength.

The evidence

(Solar Plexus Chakra - Manipura)

Visualization:

There is a flame inside you, in the center of your chest, right in the solar plexus. It is not just any flame, but a golden light that shines and moves like a sacred fire. **Every spark that rises gives you strength, every flame caresses your will.** Before you, your twin flame is reflected in the same fire. Together you face a test, a challenge that seems to impose itself between you. **You feel the weight of obstacles, but the flame within you does not waver.** Each difficulty is like wood thrown into the fire: your light grows, your will is strengthened.

The air is warm around you, the sound of flames fills the silence as the rehearsal goes on. Your skin feels the heat, and the sweat on your forehead reminds you that you are alive, full of strength. **This is the moment when your will is tested.**

Meditation:

Bring your attention to the center of the solar plexus, feeling the golden flame burning within you. **Each breath feeds the fire, makes it grow, makes it brighter.** Visualize that flame expanding, consuming every insecurity, every doubt. The heat of the flame envelops you, slowly burning away everything that holds you back. **You become aware of your personal power, your courage, your determination.** This flame is your inner power, the core of your strength.

Every breath connects you to this fire. You feel it growing, flowing through your veins, illuminating every part of you. Nothing can extinguish this light, for it is part of your essence.

Associated stone:

Hold a citrine in your hands, its surface is smooth and warm. **This stone awakens your self-confidence; it strengthens your**

worth. Whenever you feel your insecurities surfacing, hold the citrine tightly in your hand and let its energy remind you of who you are. *In those moments of doubt, let the citrine whisper in your ear, "You are powerful."*

Associated Planet:
Mars, with its energy of fire and action, propels you forward. **It is the planet of strength, will and courage.** *When Mars guides you, there is no room for fear or failure, only determination. You have the ability to face any challenge.* **The strength of Mars is within you.**

Motivational Shadow Work:
Look inside yourself and face those moments when you have reacted without thinking, those automatic behaviors that hide deep-seated insecurities. **Where is the fear of failure holding you back?** Don't turn your back on that fear; embrace it. *What is it teaching you?* **Accept the power that comes from vulnerability.** Being vulnerable does not make you weak; it makes you human. Only through this awareness can you fully ignite the fire of your personal power. **It is in your hands.**

The Separation

(Heart Chakra - Anahata)

Visualization:

You feel the emptiness in your chest, as if your heart is broken by an invisible fracture. The pain is deep, and each breath seems to bring it out even more, like a wave rising from your chest to your throat. **But in the midst of this pain, a green light begins to shine.** It is soft but powerful, enveloping that breach in the heart and beginning to fill the empty space. **That light doesn't just repair wounds, it transforms them.** Despite the separation, you feel a thin, invisible thread still binding you to your twin flame. **This bond is not one of possession, but of unconditional love.**

The air is charged with emotion, like a sweet and bitter scent together. The warmth of the green light caresses your skin, and the sound of your breath mingles with the beat of your heart, which slowly finds its rhythm again. **The pain is transformed into a feeling of openness, a doorway to healing.**

Meditation:

Close your eyes and bring your attention to the center of your chest. There, a green light begins to expand, softly, like a ray of sunshine through the leaves of the trees. **That light envelops your heart, soothing every wound, welcoming every pain without judgment.** Let the green of healing flow into you, bringing with it forgiveness: forgive yourself, forgive your twin flame. **This is the power of unconditional love.** Feel it flowing, like a slow and steady river flowing within you, fueled by compassion.

Every breath fills your chest with that green, soft, healing light. Every heartbeat expands it, spreads it to every corner of your being. **You feel the power of forgiveness flowing through you, like a balm on an open wound.**

Associated stone:
Hold a rose quartz in your hand. **Its gentle energy envelops you, reminding you that love is the key to all healing.** Whenever you feel the weight of separation crushing you, hold the rose quartz close and let its gentle but strong power guide you toward acceptance and self-love. *It is like a warm, silent embrace that envelops you when you need it most.*

Associated Planet:
The Moon, with its silvery glow, invites you to reflect. **It represents your emotions, as changeable and deep as the sea.** *In its light, you can see clearly what hurts you, but also what heals you.* **Accept the Moon as your inner guide: through reflection, you find healing.**

Motivational Shadow Work:
Face the pain of separation, without trying to escape it or cover it up. **Accept that this wound is part of your journey.** *What are you hiding behind your fear of pain?* Explore your defense mechanisms, those walls you have erected to protect yourself, and observe how they keep you away not only from others, but also from yourself. **Vulnerability is not weakness; it is the path to healing.** Only by allowing yourself to feel completely can you turn pain into growth.

Illumination

(Throat Chakra - Vishuddha)

Visualization:

A deep blue energy begins to awaken within you, in the center of your throat. **It is like a river flowing quietly, clear, but powerful.** It expands slowly, passing through every obstacle, every knot that has held back your voice for too long. **Now you can speak, without fear, without hesitation.** Every word you speak is charged with truth. **Feel how it connects you, not only with your listener, but also with yourself.** In front of you, your twin flame is there, ready to listen. **Your words are like invisible bridges stretching between your souls, connecting you on a deeper, spiritual level.**

The air around you is vibrant, as if the world itself is waiting for your words. Your throat clears, the sound of your voice is clear, every sentence that comes out is charged with sincerity, like a breath of wind dissolving the mists of the past. **This is your truth, and each word is a door opening to a more authentic connection.**

Meditation:

Close your eyes and bring your attention to the center of your throat. A bright blue light comes on, pure and clear, and begins to expand. **Each breath makes it brighter, more powerful, sweeping away all blockage, all fear.** Visualize this light opening like a flower, releasing your inner voice. **There is no more room for forced silence or unspoken words.** *Every word that emerges from this light is authentic, every silence is conscious, charged with meaning.*

Associated stone:

Hold a lapis lazuli in your hands, its cool, smooth surface reminding you of the power of truth. **This crystal connects you to your authenticity, inviting you to speak fearlessly, with**

courage and clarity. *When you feel words catch in your throat, hold the lapis lazuli tightly, and remember: truth is your strength.*

Associated planet:
Mercury guides you, with its quick, bright energy. **It is the planet of communication, of mental clarity.** *Under its influence, your words flow like clear water, and your mind opens to new understandings.* **Mercury teaches you that words have weight, but conscious silence can also be a form of profound communication.**

Shadow Work Motivational:
Reflect on the truths you've been holding back, those unspoken words stuck in your throat. **What have you been hiding from yourself?** *What secrets do you carry inside, fearing judgment or vulnerability?* Recognize the power of the words you've never spoken, but also those you've said without thinking. **Every word has an impact, every silence has meaning.** *Release what has been repressed, and discover the power that comes from your most authentic truth.* **Now is the time to speak, and also to listen carefully.**

The Gathering
(Third Eye Chakra - Ajna)

Visualization:

Your twin flame's eyes look at you, intense and deep. **Infinity is reflected in their gaze, and without a word, you feel a connection that transcends time.** In that instant, everything stops. **Through her eyes, you see the past, present and future intertwine like threads of light.** Every life you have shared, every meeting and separation, is revealed as a mosaic, fragments of a larger design. **Your third eye opens, an indigo light begins to awaken in the center of your forehead.** It is a beacon that illuminates universal truths, making you see beyond the illusion of the material world. **In this gaze, you perceive the destiny that unites you.**

The air is thick with electricity, as if everything around you is charged with meaning. Every breath is a journey, every heartbeat resonates in unison with the energy of the universe. Truths are revealed without the need for words, everything is clear, limpid, as if it has always been there, in front of you.

Meditation:

Bring your attention to the center of your forehead, where the third eye chakra pulses. **An indigo light expands, bright and powerful.** Feel how it opens, slowly, like a night flower opening under the moonlight. **This light dissolves all illusions, allows you to see beyond what is visible, beyond the surface of things.** With each breath, your intuition is enhanced, your inner vision expanded. *Now, you are able to grasp the truth hidden behind every mask.*

Associated stone:

Hold an amethyst in your hand, cold and smooth. **Its energy purifies your thoughts, enhancing your intuition and spiritual wisdom.** *When you feel that reality confuses you, that the illusions of* *the world cloud your mind, hold the amethyst close to you, and let it guide you toward clarity.*

Associated Planet:
Neptune, shrouded in mystery, represents dreams and visions. **His energy urges you to look beyond, to discover the truths that lie beneath the surface.** *In him, you find the connection between the visible and the invisible, between dream and reality. Neptune whispers secrets to you, invites you to explore the depths of your intuition.* **Do not fear what you will discover, for in those visions you will find your way.**

Motivational Shadow Work:
Look closely at the illusions you create in your mind, the distortions that keep you from the truth. **Where are you trying to control what is uncontrollable?** *What expectations have you projected onto yourself and others?* Look beyond the veil you have woven with your fears and desires. **Your intuition already knows the truth.** Even though that truth may seem uncomfortable, embrace it. **It is only by accepting the vision of your third eye that you can see your path clearly and find peace in the reunion of your souls.**

The Divine Union

(Crown Chakra - Sahasrara)

Visualization:

A pure, shimmering white light descends from above like an endless stream of energy. **It is the light of the universe calling to you, enveloping you, and uniting you with something greater.** You feel it descending from the sky, crossing the air and touching the top of your head, gently expanding into every part of your being. **In that light, you are no longer alone.** Your twin flame is beside you, and together you are immersed in this current of divine energy. **There is no separation, only unity.** All boundaries dissolve, your body and mind merge with infinity, and you *feel* that you and your twin flame are not just two souls seeking each other, but **part of one cosmic flow.**

The air is dense with light, warm and vibrant, as if every molecule around you is charged with divine energy. The sensation on your skin is that of being suspended in an endless embrace, a wave of calm and power sweeping through you completely.

Meditation:

Bring your attention to the top of your head, where the crown chakra opens. **A bright, intense white light expands above you, like a lotus flower opening out to the universe.** Each breath connects you more to universal consciousness. **You are no longer bound only to your individual existence, but part of a larger whole, an energy that expands without limits.** Let your mind dissolve into this light, abandoning all earthly thoughts, all boundaries. *You are now one with the universe, part of the divine flow that unites all things.*

Associated stone:

Hold a quartz crystal in your hands, its purity reflecting your connection to the universe. **The crystal amplifies your spiritual connection; it helps you feel that you are part of something**

greater. *When you feel separate, alone or disconnected, hold the crystal and let its energy bring you back to your oneness with the universe.*

Associated Planet:

Jupiter, the planet of expansion, invites you to grow beyond your limits. **Its energy propels you toward divine wisdom, toward the expansion of your consciousness.** *Through Jupiter, you discover that there is no end to your path of spiritual growth; every moment is a new opportunity to expand and connect to the divine.*

Motivational Shadow Work:

Look deep inside and observe the sense of separation you often feel from the universe. **Where do you feel the need for control?** *What fears hold you back from fully surrendering to the cosmic current?* **Accept that you are part of a greater design, that union with the divine comes when you shed the idea of perfection.** Your perfection is in your imperfection, in your complete acceptance of who you are. *Only when you let go of control do you find true freedom and true union with the universe.*

FINAL REFLECTIONS

Are you ready to meet your twin flame? This question may resonate within you like a mysterious call. Is there a part of you that feels the pull of such a deep experience, that makes your heart beat faster? Or perhaps you are still uncertain, poised between the desire to know it and the fear of the intensity it brings. Whatever stage you are in, this book is here to accompany you. **It is a guide designed to illuminate the path, to give you the clarity you need**. Whether you are trying to understand who, among the people around you, is in your life for a specific reason, or who will be by your side forever, your spiritual growth is intertwined with your journey toward more authentic love.

Every relationship you create has a purpose. Some people help you grow, others are here to teach you difficult lessons, while some represent the soul that mirrors you. **Always remember that the universe speaks to you in subtle ways, through signs, insights, and synchronicities.** And when you are ready, those signs will guide you to your twin flame.

The real secret is to rely on the journey. **Don't rush anything, let the universe show you the way.** Keep looking, keep reading the signs, and with each step you will feel your awareness growing.

Good luck with every choice you make. **Your twin flame is waiting for you, even if you don't yet know when you will meet.** And when that time comes, you will know that every experience you have had has prepared you to recognize that eternal bond.

132

GLOSSARY OF TERMS

Twin Flame - The other half of your soul, a soul divided into two incarnations.

Soul Mate - A soul with whom one shares deep spiritual and karmic connections, but not necessarily the twin flame.

Spiritual Awakening-The process by which one connects to one's spiritual essence.

Ascension - Elevation of the level of consciousness and spiritual vibration.

Heart Chakra - The energy center related to unconditional love, central to the path of twin flames.

Christ Consciousness - Higher level of consciousness, related to unconditional love.

Karma - The set of actions and experiences accumulated in past lives that affect the current path.

Dharmic - Related to the soul's mission in fulfilling its destiny.

Telepathic Connection - The ability to communicate without words with one's twin flame.

Synchronicity - Significant coincidences that indicate you are on the right path.

Ego - The part of self related to individual identity, often at odds with the soul.

Illusion of Separation - The belief that one is separated from one's twin flame.

Union-The moment when the twin flames are reunited both spiritually and physically.

Running and Chasing - The dynamic in which one twin flame runs away (runner) while the other chases after it (chaser).

Karmic Soul - A person with whom you have a connection to resolve debts or karmic lessons.

Energetic Resonance - The energetic vibration that two souls emit in tune with each other.

Soul Mission-The divine purpose that a soul is called to fulfill during its existence.

Vibration-The energy level at which a person vibrates, affecting his or her reality.

Soul Contract - A spiritual agreement made between souls before incarnation, relating to life experiences.

Spiritual Healing-The process of purifying and transforming the soul to reach a higher level.

Divine Feminine Energy - The energy related to creativity, intuition and spiritual nourishment.

Divine Masculine Energy- The energy related to action, protection and structure.

Energy Purification-The process of removing negative or toxic energies from the energy field.

Fusion of Souls - The spiritual and energetic integration between the twin flames.

Energy Fields-The auras and chakras that represent a person's life energy field.

Crown Chakra - The energy center that connects the soul to universal wisdom.

Shadow Work - The practice of confronting and healing the repressed and dark aspects of one's self.

Duality-The concept of opposites (light/shadow, good/evil) found in the universe and in human relationships.

Unity-The state of connectedness and wholeness with the whole.

Through the Heart - Acting and thinking with unconditional love, guided by the heart chakra.

Manifestation-The process by which what is desired is attracted and materialized.

Energy Grid-The invisible network of energy that connects all souls and the cosmos.

Spiritual Alchemy - The transformation of the soul through inner processes, as in the journey of twin flames.

Enlightenment - The attainment of a higher state of spiritual awareness.

Soul Recognition-The moment when you recognize your twin flame.

Past Life - Experiences of previous existences that influence the present.

Divine Purpose - The sacred mission that every soul is called to fulfill.

Karmic Cycle - The cycle of life experiences needed to resolve karmic lessons.

Energy Protection-The practice of shielding one's energy field from negative influences.

Unity Consciousness-Awareness of being part of an interconnected whole.

Spiritual Guide - Spiritual beings or entities that offer support and advice along the way.

Divine **Trust** - Total surrender to the divine will in the path of the twin flames.

Ancient Soul - A soul that has experienced many incarnations and accumulated wisdom.

Shadow - The hidden and unaccepted aspects of ourselves.

Test - The spiritual trials a twin flame must face in order to grow.

Cycle of Rebirth-The process of spiritual death and rebirth.

Energy Portal - A temporal opening in which cosmic energy is amplified.

Aura - The energy field that surrounds and protects the physical body.

Intuition - The inner wisdom that guides the soul.

Opening of the Heart-The process of receiving love and healing at the level of the heart.

Transmigration of Souls - The soul's journey through different lives and planes of existence.

Spiritual Retreat - A period of isolation to connect with one's soul.

Meditation-The practice of quieting the mind to connect with one's higher self.

Energetic Integration - The harmonious union of divine male and female energies.

Unconditional Love - A pure and unconditional love.

Out-of-Body Experiences - Experiences of astral travel or connection with other planes of existence.

Channeling-The practice of receiving spiritual messages from higher entities.

Call to Action - The impulse that drives the twin flames to fulfill their mission.

Signals from the Universe - Messages the universe sends to guide you on the spiritual path.

Contrast - The challenges that strengthen the soul and prepare it for union.

Inner Vision-The ability to see beyond the physical world through intuition.

Own Love - The act of loving and accepting oneself completely.

Lunar Cycle-The link between the moon cycle and the spiritual path.

Rooting-The process of connecting to the earth to maintain energy balance.

Reversal of Roles-Changes in energy roles between runner and pursuer.

Call of the Soul - The call that urges a twin flame to follow its own path.

Spiritual Mirror - The twin flame reflects your hidden aspects and inner wounds.

Opening of the Third Eye-The activation of the chakra that enables perception of higher realities.

Divine Truth-The higher knowledge underlying universal existence.

Universal Connection - The awareness of being an integral part of the universe.

Sacred Love - Love that goes beyond physical, spiritual and divine attraction.

Cycle of Separation-The phase in which the twin flames move apart to heal separately.

Reunion-The return of the twin flames in harmonious union.

Desire of the Soul - The deep urge to reunite with one's twin flame.

Karmic Healing - The release of old karmic debts.

Memory of the Soul - The deep memories stored by the soul of past lives and lessons.

Inner Truth-The deepest and most authentic awareness of self.

Prophecy of the Soul - The spiritual vision of a soul's destiny.

Surrender - The release of control to rely on the guidance of the universe.

Healer's Path - The call to heal self and others through divine love.

Energy Portals-Phases or places that accelerate spiritual growth.

Sidereal Connection - The connection with cosmic energy and the stars.

Divine Time-The perfect moment orchestrated by the universe for experiences.

Energetic Resistance - Energy blocks that prevent the twin flames from coming together.

Soul Sharing - The spiritual and vibratory fusion between twin flames.

Spiritual Blossoming-The complete awakening and development of one's divine potential.

Karmic Clash - A conflict that arises to resolve old karmic lessons.

Energy Flow-The natural movement of energies between the twin flames.

Karma release-The process of dissolving negative karmic bonds.

Spiritual Purification - Soul cleansing through sacred practices.

Dream Vision - Dreams or prophetic visions related to the twin flame.

Alignment-The state of balance and harmony between mind, body and spirit.

Planetary Consciousness-The level of collective awareness on a global scale.

Spiritual Initiation - A sacred passage that leads to a new level of spiritual understanding.

Evolution of the Soul-The progressive growth of the soul toward higher states.

Divine Contract - A sacred covenant made by the soul before incarnation.

Twin Portal - An energy passage that accelerates the path of twin flames.

Divine Protection-The protection received from

higher forces during the spiritual journey.

Self-love - The practice of self-acceptance and self-respect.

Healing the Heart - The process of releasing emotional wounds to open up to love.

Bibliographical references
and recommended readings

- **Evolutionary Esoteric Numerology** - Templum Dianae Media - 2023
- **The Numbers of Angels** - Templum Dianae Media - 2023